研究生英语系列教材

English for Professional Master's Degree Candidates (Second Edition)

专业硕士研究生英语

（第二版）

主编　王爱华　李淑静

编者　程　英　李淑静　陆蓉蕾　王爱华

英文审校　Sheryl Smalligan（美国）

北京大学出版社

PEKING UNIVERSITY PRESS

图书在版编目(CIP)数据

专业硕士研究生英语/王爱华,李淑静主编. —2版. —北京:北京大学出版社,2018.8
(研究生英语系列教材)
ISBN 978-7-301-29744-5

Ⅰ.①专… Ⅱ.①王…②李… Ⅲ.①英语—研究生—教材 Ⅳ.①H319.39

中国版本图书馆CIP数据核字(2018)第176503号

书　　　名	专业硕士研究生英语(第二版)
	ZHUANYE SHUOSHI YANJIUSHENG YINGYU
著作责任者	王爱华　李淑静　主编
责任编辑	黄瑞明　李　娜
标准书号	ISBN 978-7-301-29744-5
出版发行	北京大学出版社
地　　　址	北京市海淀区成府路205号　100871
网　　　址	http://www.pup.cn　新浪微博:@北京大学出版社
电子信箱	zpup@pup.pku.edu.cn
电　　　话	邮购部 62752015　发行部 62750672　编辑部 62759634
印　刷　者	河北滦县鑫华书刊印刷厂
经　销　者	新华书店
	720毫米×1020毫米　16开本　7.75印张　300千字
	2008年1月第1版　2018年8月第2版　2024年7月第7次印刷
定　　　价	35.00元

未经许可,不得以任何方式复制或抄袭本书之部分或全部内容。
版权所有,侵权必究
举报电话:010-62752024　电子信箱:fd@pup.pku.edu.cn
图书如有印装质量问题,请与出版部联系,电话:010-62756370

修订说明

《专业硕士研究生英语》自2007年首次出版以来,一直在非专业硕士研究生英语教学中使用。此教材选材精良,主题恰当。练习安排较为合理。学生比较喜欢其中的文章。但在使用过程中,我们也发现有些单元内容过于容易,有些单元内容过难。而随着时间发展,有些切合当时社会的主题发生了一些变化。因此,为使这部教材更为完善,更适应新形势的教学需要,我们对这本书进行了如下修订:

一、首先,原书包含了过多的单元。此次,我们对原书进行了精简。删除了过难、过易的单元,也删除了主题稍显过时的单元。新增加了一个体现与新兴的互联网有关的网络文化的单元。希望学生们能对在强大的网络信息发展的前提下如何保护好自我进行思索。

二、单元的顺序也进行了调整。从难易程度上、从主题上重新调整了单元顺序。将表现励志的、充满正能量的、表现家庭亲情的文章放在前面。如第一单元是关于如何摆正自己在人生、在社会的位置以及在现代社会中如何看待英雄在我们生活中的楷模作用。第二单元体现了父子、父女亲情和父母对于我们人生的指导。将原来较难的第二单元放到了后面。

三、保留的单元中,对部分课文也进行了替换。第一单元关于英雄的文章是新选的。第六单元,关于美国对全球文化的影响的单元,替换了原来的副课文,新选的文章体现的是越来越多的美国移民倾向于返回自己母国的潮流。

四、删除了一些过于容易的练习;合并了一些练习;对于一些原有的练习也进行了替换更改;删除了语法练习和翻译课文的练习。

五、修订版新增加了实用英语写作的内容,此部分内容是编者从多本关于英语写作的原著中提取重要内容改编而成,由于我们面向的学生很多来自于工作岗位,用英语发邮件、写公文信函,在工作岗位用英语写报告、备忘录、会议纪要、建议书等都非常必要。因此我们增加了这项与他们实际要求紧密相关的内容。每一专题都附有相关模板,对于学生实际应用英语有很大帮助。

六、纠正了原书中的错误,并对书中不妥之处做了较为细致的修改。

本书由长期从事非英语专业研究生英语教学的北京大学王爱华副教授、李淑静副教授修订。由北京大学博士生英语教学专家Louise Jansen担任审校。

本书的编写和出版得到了北京大学2016年度教材建设立项的资助以及责任编辑黄瑞明老师的宝贵意见,在此谨表示衷心感谢。由于编写仓促,缺点在所难免,我们诚挚地希望使用本教材的师生和读者提出批评和建议,以便今后改进和完善。

王爱华　李淑静
2018年5月于北京

前　言

随着我国各层次、各类型研究生教育的开展,英语教学中把一种教材用于所有研究生的做法已不能适应新的形势。为了照顾不同类型不同层次的研究生学习英语的不同需求和特点,真正贯彻因材施教的教育思想,我们以专业硕士学位研究生和各类研究生课程班学生为主要目标读者,编写了这本教材,在课文长度、难度和练习形式上区别于全日制硕士研究生的教材。

作为研究生的英语教材,本书力求做到内容新颖,知识性思想性强,渗透对文化的学习、思考和探究,并能体现学术性。同时,语言首先是交际工具,非英语专业研究生掌握英语的目的是为了应用,因此本书还十分注重语言的实用性和选材的广泛性、时代性。

本书以课文阅读为核心,通过多样化的练习,对学生进行语言知识(如词汇、句型扩展及语法巩固)和读、说、写、译等语言技能的综合训练,提高学生的英语应用能力,从而达到学以致用的目的。

我们从教学实际出发,编写了可在24至48学时内完成的教学内容。全书共12单元,每个单元都有相同题材的主课文和副课文各一篇,以保证足够的阅读量,但是语言知识和技能的训练围绕主课文展开。具体编排模式如下:

Pre-reading Activities: 读前活动。以知识性或经验性问题引出主课文话题,或是提问课文中个别关键词句的意义,以激发学生的阅读兴趣,同时可作为口语活动主题。

Text: 课文。

Notes: 课文注释。对课文中涉及的人物、地点、事件、组织名称、典故、俚语等进行详细的双语解释。

Vocabulary: 词汇。选取50个左右的词语,注以国际音标并双语解释其在课文语境中的特定意义。

Useful Expressions: 实用短语表达。对课文中出现的常用动词词组、介词词组及其他表达法进行英文释义和举例。

Topics for Discussion: 读后讨论话题。问题是开放性的,供师生结合课文进行深度讨论时参考,也可作为口头表达或书面表达的题目使用。

Exercises: 练习。该部分分成以下几项内容:

A. 阅读理解:用提问、选择正确答案、判断正误等不同形式帮助学生从中心思想和细节两个方面深入、准确地理解课文内容。

B. 课文原词填空:引导学生注意学习模仿原文的地道语言。

C. 语法复习:复习课文涉及到的重点语法知识。

D-F. 填空:分别单项操练课文中的重点词汇、词组、表达法。

G. 综合填空:融会对学生语法、词汇、篇章知识的综合考查。

H. 汉译英练习:重点操练课文中出现的词组。

I. 英译汉练习:重点翻译课文的某些段落。

Suggestions for Writing: 短文写作练习。通常包括写课文小结、评论课文中某个观点、模仿课文结构写作等几种形式,为半控制性写作任务。

与本书配套出版的还有《专业硕士研究生英语自学手册》。书中有练习参考答案、难句注释及翻译、模拟试题等,供自学的同学检查学习效果。

本书由长期从事非英语专业研究生英语教学的北京大学李淑静副教授、华东师范大学金衡山副教授担任主编,由北京大学博士生英语教学负责人、美籍专家Sheryl Smalligan担任审校,其他参编者也都是研究生英语教学一线的骨干教师,分别来自北京大学、北京理工大学和北京第二外国语大学。

本书的编写和出版得到了北京大学2006年度教材建设立项的资助以及责任编辑徐万丽老师的宝贵意见,在此谨表示衷心感谢。由于编写仓促,缺点在所难免,我们诚挚地希望使用本教材的师生和读者提出批评和建议,以便今后修订时改进和完善。

编 者
2006年11月于北京

Contents

Unit One ··· 1
    Text A   The Right to Fail ································· 1
    Text B   About Heroes ······································ 12

Unit Two ··· 18
    Text A   Any More Like You at Home? ················ 18
    Text B   Only Daughter ···································· 32

Unit Three ·· 39
    Text A   Propaganda Techniques in Advertising ········ 39
    Text B   With These Words I Can Sell You Anything ······ 52

Unit Four ·· 60
    Text A   How to Deal with a Difficult Boss ············· 60
    Text B   Bad Bosses and How to Handle Them ········· 73

Unit Five ··· 81
    Text A   A Granddaughter's Fear ························· 81
    Text B   Stay Young ·· 92

Unit Six ·· 100
    Text A   That Lean and Hungry Look ··················· 100
    Text B   Neat People vs. Sloppy People ················· 110

Unit One

Text A

Pre-reading Activities

1. You are going to read a text about "dropping out"—leaving school or college before graduating. What are the disadvantages of dropping out of college?
2. The author of the text takes a positive stance on dropouts in the sense that dropping out can be constructive to one's self-development. How could that be?
3. In order to support his point of view, Zinsser points to several eminent dropouts. Who are they and in what ways have they been successful?
4. What advice would you give a friend with high intellectual ability who wants to drop out of college?
5. The following sentences are taken from the text. What do they mean?
   "For the young, dropping out is often a way to dropping in."
   "Countless people have had a bout with it and come out stronger as a result. Many have even come out famous."
   "Obviously it's better to succeed than to flop. And in general a long education is more helpful than a short one."

The Right to Fail
William Zinsser[1]

1. I like "dropout" as an addition to the American language because it's brief and it's clear. What I don't like is that we use it almost entirely as a dirty word.

2. We only apply it to people under twenty-one. Yet an adult who spends his days and nights watching mindless TV programs is more of a dropout than an eighteen-year-old who quits college, with its frequently mindless courses, to become, say, a **VISTA**[2] volunteer. For the young, dropping out is often a way to dropping in.

3. To hold this opinion, however, is little short of treason in America. A boy or girl who leaves college is branded a failure—and the right to fail is one of the few freedoms that this country does not grant its citizens. The American dream is a dream of "getting ahead," painted in strokes of gold wherever we look. Our advertisements and TV commercials are a hymn to material success, our magazines and articles a toast to people who made it to the

top. Smoke the right cigarette or drive the right car—so the ads imply—and girls will be swooning into your deodorized arms or caressing your expensive lapels. Happiness goes to the man who has the sweet smell of achievement. He is our national idol, and everybody else is our national fink.

4 I want to put in a word for the fink, especially the teen-age fink, because if we give him time to get through his finkdom—if we release him from the pressure of attaining certain goals by a certain age—he has a good chance of becoming our national idol, a **Jefferson**③ or a **Thoreau**④, a **Buckminster Fuller**⑤ or an **Adlai Stevenson**⑥, a man with a mind of his own. We need mavericks and dissenters and dreamers far more than we need junior vice-presidents, but we paralyze them by insisting that every step be a step up to the next rung of the ladder. Yet in the fluid years of youth, the only way for boys and girls to find their proper road is often to take a hundred side trips, poking out in different directions, faltering, drawing back, and starting again.

5 "But what if I fail?" they ask, whispering the dreadful word across the Generation Gap to their parents, who are back home at the Establishment nursing their "middle-class values" and cultivating their "goal-oriented society." The parents whisper back "Don't."

6 What they should say is "Don't be afraid to fail!" Failure isn't fatal. Countless people have had a bout with it and come out stronger as a result. Many have even come out famous. History is strewn with eminent dropouts, "loners" who followed their own trail, not worrying about its odd twists and turns because they had faith in their own sense of direction. To read their biographies is always exhilarating, not only because they beat the system, but because their system was better than the one they beat.

7 Luckily, such rebels still turn up often enough to prove that individualism, though badly threatened, is not extinct. Much has been written, for instance, about the fitful scholastic career of Thomas P. F. Hoving, New York's former **Parks Commissioner**⑦ and now director of the **Metropolitan Museum of Art**⑧. Hoving was a dropout's dropout, entering and leaving schools as if they were motels, often at the request of the management. Still, he must have learned something during those unorthodox years, for he dropped in again at the top of his profession.

8 His case reminds me of another boyhood—that of Holden Caulfield in J. D. Salinger's **The Catcher in the Rye**⑨, the most popular literary hero of the postwar period. There is nothing accidental about the grip that this dropout continues to hold on the affections of an entire American generation. Nobody else, real or invented, has made such an engaging shambles of our "goal-oriented society," so gratified our secret belief that the "phonies" are in power and the good guys up the creek. Whether Holden has also reached the top of his chosen field today is one of those speculations that delight fanciers of good fiction. I speculate that he has. **Holden Caulfield**⑩, incidentally, is now thirty-six.

9 I'm not urging everyone to go out and fail just for the sheer therapy of it, or to quit college just to coddle some vague discontent. Obviously it's better to succeed than to flop. And in general a long education is more helpful than a short one. (Thanks to my education,

for example, I can tell **George Eliot**[11] from **T. S. Eliot**[12], I can handle the pluperfect tense in French, and I know that Caesar beat the **Helvetii**[13] because he had enough *frumentum*.) I only mean that failure isn't bad in itself, or success automatically good.

10 Fred Zinnemann, who has directed some of Hollywood's most honored movies, was asked by a reporter, when *A Man for All Seasons* won every prize, about his previous film, *Behold a Pale Horse*, which was a box-office disaster. "I don't feel any obligation to be successful," Zinnemann replied. "Success can be dangerous—you feel you know it all. I've learned a great deal from my failures." A similar point was made by Richard Brooks about his ambitious money loser, *Lord Jim*. Recalling the three years of his life that went into it, talking almost with elation about troubles that befell his unit in Cambodia, Brooks told me that he learned more about his craft from this considerable failure than from his many earlier hits.

11 It's a point, of course, that applies throughout the arts. Writers, playwrights, painters, and composers work in the expectation of periodic defeat, but they wouldn't keep going back into the arena if they thought it was the end of the world. It isn't the end of the world. For an artist—and perhaps for anybody—it is the only way to grow.

12 Today's younger generation seems to know that this is true, seems willing to take the risks in life that artists take in art. "Society," needless to say, still has the upper hand—it sets the goals and condemns as a failure everybody who won't play. But the dropouts and the hippies are not as afraid of failure as their parents and grandparents. This could mean, as their elders might say, that they are just plumb lazy, secure in the comforts of an affluent state. It could also mean, however, that they just don't buy the old standards of success and are rapidly writing new ones.

13 Recently it was announced, for instance, that more than two hundred thousand Americans have inquired about service in VISTA (the domestic Peace Corps) and that, according to a **Gallup survey**[14], "more than three million American college students would serve VISTA in some capacity if given the opportunity." This is hardly the road to riches or to an executive suite. Yet I have met many of these young volunteers, and they are not pining for traditional success. On the contrary, they appear more fulfilled than the average vice-president with a swimming pool.

14 Who is to say, then, if there is any right path to the top, or even to say what the top consists of? Obviously the colleges don't have more than a partial answer—otherwise the young would not be so disaffected with an education that they consider vapid. Obviously business does not have the answer—otherwise the young would not be so scornful of its call to be an **organization man**[15].

15 The fact is, nobody has the answer, and the dawning awareness of this fact seems to me one of the best things happening in America today. Success and failure are again becoming individual vision, as they were when the country was younger, not rigid categories. Maybe we are learning again to cherish this right of everyone to succeed on his own terms and to fail as often as necessary along the way.

Notes

① **William K. Zinsser** (1922—)　American critic and writer, born in New York and educated at Princeton. A columnist for *Look* and *Life*, he has been on the faculty of Yale University since 1970. His books include *Pop Goes America* (1966), *The Lunacy Boom* (1970), *On Writing Well* (1980), and *Writing with a Word Processor* (1983). Zinsser opposes the common view of the college dropout as someone who at best will emerge as a "late bloomer" and at worst will be stuck on the sidelines of success. In fact, he points out, dropping out may be a prelude to greater awareness and more purposeful ambition. It may simply be the sign of a ruggedly individualistic nature. 威廉·津泽（美国作家）

② **VISTA**　Volunteers In Service To America, United States government-sponsored program which places individuals with community-based agencies to help find long-term solutions to the problems caused by urban and rural poverty. Since 1965, over 120,000 Americans have performed national service as VISTA Volunteers. 美国服务志愿队

③ **Thomas Jefferson** (1743—1826)　third president of the United States (1801—1809), author of the *Declaration of Independence*, and apostle of agrarian democracy. 托马斯·杰斐逊（美国第三任总统）

④ **Henry David Thoreau** (1817—1862)　American philosopher and writer, most famous for his work *Walden*, the chronicle of his two-year, two-month, and two-day stay at Walden Pond in a cabin he had built with his own hands. 亨利·大卫·梭罗（美国作家、哲学家，著有《瓦尔登湖》）

⑤ **Richard Buckminster "Bucky" Fuller** (1895—1983)　American visionary designer, architect, and inventor. He was also a professor at Southern Illinois University and a prolific writer. Fuller was most famous for his geodesic domes, which can be seen as part of military radar stations, civic buildings, and exhibition attractions. 理查德·巴克明斯特·富勒（美国建筑师，以发明测地线拱顶而闻名）

⑥ **Adlai Ewing Stevenson** (1900—1965)　politician and diplomat, twice the Democratic Party's candidate for President of the United States. He brought a freshness, a depth, passion, wit, and vision to American politics and to international diplomatic discourse that illumined an era. Many considered him one of the greatest political orators of his time, second only to Winston Churchill. 阿德雷·E. 斯蒂文森（美国著名政治家，曾两度当选民主党自由派总统候选人，影响了美国人讨论公共事务的方式）

⑦ **Parks Commissioner**　the official in charge of the New York City Department of Parks and Recreation, whose job includes improving park facilities and programs for children, developing new waterfront parks and greenways, and making New York City bloom with millions of new flowers and hundreds of gardens. 美国纽约公园管理部门负责人

⑧ **Metropolitan Museum of Art**　There are several large museums in New York but the Metropolitan Museum of Art is truly gigantic. From the sidewalk on Fifth Avenue, the Met, with its tall columns and windows, immense stairways and water fountains, looks like an emperor's palace. The size and diversity of the collection on display is even more impressive. The museum collection contains works from every part of the world, spanning the Stone Age to the twentieth century. 美国纽约大都会艺术博物馆

⑨ **The Catcher in the Rye**   Although *The Catcher in the Rye*, by J. D. Salinger, caused considerable controversy when it was first published in 1951, the book—the account of three disoriented days in the life of a troubled sixteen-year-old boy—was an instant hit. Within two weeks after its release, it was listed number one on The New York *Times* best-seller list, and it stayed there for thirty weeks. It remained immensely popular for many years, especially among teenagers and young adults, largely because of its fresh, brash style and anti-establishment attitudes—typical attributes of many people emerging from the physical and psychological turmoil of adolescence. 《麦田守望者》(美国作家塞林格著)

⑩ **Holden Caulfield**   The first-person narrator of *The Catcher in the Rye*, Holden Caulfield is the sixteen-year-old son of wealthy New York parents. His defining characteristic is his hatred of "phoniness" in every sphere of life. In fact, the prevalence of phonies in academia is one reason why Holden has just flunked out of his third prep school, Pencey, when the novel opens. Despite emerging as a great iconoclastic rebel, Holden also lacks direction, and that is reflected in his three days of wandering around New York. 《麦田守望者》中的自述主人公

⑪ **George Eliot** (1819—1880)   Victorian writer and humane freethinker, whose insightful psychological novels paved the way to modern character portrayals — contemporary of Dostoevsky (1821—1881) who at the same time in Russia developed similar narrative techniques. 乔治·艾略特(英国维多利亚时期女作家)

⑫ **T. S. Eliot** (1888—1965)   American poet and playwright, who lived in England for most of his life. He is one of the most important writers of the twentieth century and won the Nobel Prize for Literature in 1948. His works include *The Cocktail Party*, *The Waste Land*, and "The Love Song of J. Alfred Prufrock." T. S. 艾略特(美国诗人、剧作家，1948年诺贝尔文学奖得主)

⑬ **Helvetii**   also the Celtic Helvetii, thought to be the first permanent settlers of Switzerland and southern Germany in about the second century BC. About a century later, the Romans realized the commercial and strategic importance of this area and Gaius Julius Caesar (100—44 BC), Roman general and statesman who laid the foundations of the Roman imperial system, conquered it in 58 BC. 赫尔维蒂人(凯尔特民族)

⑭ **Gallup survey (poll)**   a random sampling of what most people think about an issue by asking a number of them questions, especially in order to find out how they will vote in an election. The Gallup Organization conducts many such polls. 盖洛普民意调查

⑮ **organization man**   In 1956 William H. Whyte wrote *The Organization Man*, which argued that people not only worked for organizations but that they were shaped by them as well. 商业作家小威廉·H. 怀特认为，组织中的男性需要一种既定的、稳定的和边缘化的生存方式；个人观点的表达要修剪得像郊外的草坪那样短，这些就是企业中的男人。在他的畅销书，后来成为经典的《企业人》(*The Organization Man*)中，他悲叹粗犷的个人主义者的

消失,在他周围的员工更多的是受到"压力"的驱使。这些人"毫不起眼,并没有过多的热情",他们的未来被人推来揉去,受到一些自己不能左右的因素的控制。

Vocabulary

1. treason [ˈtriːzən] *n.* the crime of being disloyal to one's country or its government, especially by helping its enemies or trying to overthrow it, 通敌(罪), 叛国(罪)
2. stroke [strəʊk] *n.* a single movement of a pen or brush in writing or painting, 一笔, 一画
3. hymn [hɪm] *n.* a song of praise to a deity, 圣诗, 赞美歌
4. deodorize [diːˈəʊdəraɪz] *vt. also* deodorise 〈*British*〉, to remove a bad smell or to make it less noticeable, 除去……的臭气
5. caress [kəˈres] *vt.* to touch someone gently and lovingly, 爱抚, 抚摸
6. lapel [ləˈpel] *n.* the part of a coat or jacket front that is joined to the collar and folded back on each side, (西服上衣或夹克的)翻领
7. fink [fɪŋk] *n.* a person deserving scorn, 卑鄙的家伙, 讨厌鬼
8. maverick [ˈmævərɪk] *n.* a person who behaves and thinks differently from most and yet is often successful, 持不同意见者, 标新立异的人
9. dissenter [dɪˈsentə] *n.* a person or organization that disagrees with an official decision or accepted opinion, 反对者
10. paralyze [ˈpærəlaɪz] *vt.* to disable, to make ineffective; to render incapable of movement, 使无能为力
11. rung [rʌŋ] *n.* the wooden or metal bars that form the steps on a ladder, 梯级
12. fluid [ˈfluːɪd] *adj.* unsettled, not fixed, 不固定的, 易变的
13. falter [ˈfɔːltə] *vt.* to hesitate or pause because of fear or weakness, 蹒跚, 踉跄
14. Establishment [ɪˈstæblɪʃmənt] *n.* the group of people in a society or profession who have a lot of power and influence and are often opposed to change or new ideas, 现存体制; 当权人物, 有权势人物
15. bout [baʊt] *n.* a short period of intense activity, 一阵, 一次
16. unorthodox [ʌnˈɔːθədɒks] *adj.* different from what is usual or accepted by most people, 非正统的, 非常规的
17. shambles [ˈʃæmbəlz] *n.* complete disorder and confusion, 凌乱, 杂乱无章
18. phony [ˈfəʊnɪ] *n.* someone who pretends to be something he or she is not, 骗子, 冒牌货
19. coddle [kɒdl] *vt.* to be overly protective and indulgent, 溺爱, 娇惯
20. therapy [ˈθerəpɪ] *n.* the treatment of an illness or injury over a fairly long period of time, (尤指不用药物或不做手术的)疗法
21. flop [flɒp] *vi.* to fail totally and utterly, 失败
22. pluperfect [pluːˈpɜːfɪkt] *n.* (technical) the past perfect tense of a verb, 过去完成时
23. *frumentum* [fruːˈmentəm] *n. Latin* a cereal crop, 谷类作物
24. befall [bɪˈfɔːl] *vt.* to happen to, 注定降临, 发生

25. hippie [ˈhɪpɪ] *n.* someone, especially in the 1960s, who opposed violence and adopted "counter culture" dress and lifestyles, 嬉皮士
26. elation [ɪˈleɪʃən] *n.* great happiness and excitement, 兴高采烈
27. suite [swiːt] *n.* group of rooms related in function, 套房
28. disaffected [ˌdɪsəˈfektɪd] *adj.* not satisfied with one's government or leaders and therefore no longer supportive, 不忠的, 不满的
29. vapid [ˈvæpɪd] *adj.* lacking intelligence, interest, or imagination, 毫无生气的, 乏味的

Useful Expressions

1. **be little short of:** used to emphasize how great or extreme something is
    (1) The results are nothing short of magnificent.
    (2) On the strength of this collection, his current lack of fans is little short of a tragedy.
2. **get ahead:** to be more successful than other people in similar circumtances
    (1) Which just goes to prove—you do have to be a somebody to get ahead in this town!
    (2) The flattening of organizations means that all employees have to learn that old-fashioned promotion is not the only way of getting ahead.
3. **put in a good word for:** to help someone achieve something by recommending him or her to someone else
    (1) I'll put in a good word for you with the management.
    (2) He put in a good word for him at meetings of the Jockey Club.
4. **poke out:** to extend out or through
    (1) Ella looked at the tiny face poking out of the blanket.
    (2) A young doctor poked his head out and called me into the examination room.
5. **draw back:** to move backwards, especially in fear or surprise
    (1) She peeped into the box and drew back in horror.
    (2) In the end the government drew back from their extreme standpoint.
6. **be strewn with:** to be scattered with
    (1) The street was strewn with broken glass.
    (2) Lafayette Square was strewn with the stuff of deconstruction: moving vans, cherry pickers, lumber, and paper.
7. **turn up:** to be found, especially by chance, after having been lost or searched for
    (1) Eventually my watch turned up in a coat pocket.
    (2) After seven months on the case, no real clues turned up.
8. **be up the creek:** to be in a very difficult situation
    (1) I'll really be up the creek if I don't get paid this week.
    (2) Chairmen of football clubs are in the papers and on the radio only when the team is up the creek.

9. **in itself:** considered separately from any other facts
   (1) This awareness, in itself, is believed to generate sufficient grief to restore and ensure cooperation.
   (2) The planning becomes an end in itself.
10. **in the expectation of:** in the hope that something will happen
    (1) Anne left Germany in the expectation of seeing her family again before very long.
    (2) He spent money lavishly in the expectation of receiving a large inheritance.
11. **have the upper hand:** to have a position of advantage; control
    (1) Police have gained the upper hand over the drug dealers in the area.
    (2) After hours of fierce negotiation, the president gained the upper hand.
12. **the road to:** headed toward something
    (1) It was the first step along the road to democracy.
    (2) Now is the time for tonics to help us forget the pain and step out on the road to recovery.
13. **on one's own terms:** according to the conditions that someone determines for themselves
    (1) He wanted our relationship to be only on his terms.
    (2) If I agree to do it, it will be on my own terms.

Understanding the Text

1. What two sides of society are pitted against each other in this essay? On which side is the author?
2. What is Zinsser's definition of "dropout"? How is it different from the Establishment's definition?
3. What does the title mean?
4. Which sentence in the opening paragraphs of the author's argument best states his thesis?
5. In Paragraph 6 the author argues that people should not be afraid to fail. Why does he say this?
6. In which paragraph does the author explain that he does not consider failure a goal in itself?
7. Obviously Fred Zinnemann and Richard Brooks are not college dropouts. Why does the author mention them?
8. According to Zinsser, what is the path to success?
9. What is the function of the last sentence?

Exercises

A. Fill in the blanks with the appropriate words from the text.

1. The author's opinion is little short of _____ in America where boys and girls who leave

college are _____ a failure, given that the country does not grant its citizens the right to _____. The American dream is a dream of "getting ahead," painted in _____ wherever we look. Our advertisements and TV commercials are a _____ to material success, our magazine articles a _____ to people who made it to the top.

2. The author wants to put in a word for the _____ because if we release him from the pressure of _____ certain goals, he has a good _____ of becoming our national _____ or a person with a mind of his own.

3. Due to _____, parents do not understand their children and they just urge them to accept _____ and cultivate their _____.

B. Choose from the words given below to complete the following sentences, changing the word form where necessary.

| brief | apply | quit | paralyze | nurse | attain |
| beat | accidental | incidentally | urge | fulfill | vision |

1. He had a clear _____ of how he hoped the company would develop.
2. The offer only _____ to flights from London and Manchester.
3. Fear of unemployment is _____ the economy.
4. It is better not to extend what was, after all, an _____ and purely professional relationship.
5. He _____ his job after an argument with a colleague.
6. For years he _____ a grievance against his former employer.
7. The book begins with a _____ outline of the history of modern China.
8. Accountants know a few ways to _____ the system.
9. She _____ me to go out on my own, to start my own company.
10. After a year she _____ her ideal weight.
11. Visiting Disneyland _____ a boyhood dream.
12. The wine, _____, goes very well with a mature cheese.

C. Fill in the blanks with the phrases given below, changing the form where necessary.

get ahead	be little short of
put in a (good word) for	hold on
poke out	be up the creek
come out	in itself
be strewn with	make a point
turn up	take the risk(s)
draw back	

1. The results _____ astonishing.
2. In the end the government _____ from their extreme standpoint.
3. His room _____ books and papers.
4. If I don't get my passport by Friday, I'll _____.

5. There is a slight infection in the lung which _____ is not serious.
6. Many people are willing to _____ in order to protect their families.
7. I'd almost given up hope of finding a house I liked, and then suddenly this one _____.
8. Ella looked at the tiny face _____ of the blanket.
9. She soon found that it wasn't easy to _____ in the movie business.
10. I got the job because Paul _____ for me.

D. Fill in the blanks with the expressions given below, changing the form where necessary.

on...terms	far more than	a way to
a good chance of	the upper hand	who's to say
who is to say	twists and turns	the road to
in power	dropout	in the expectation of

1. He allowed this to continue _____ eventual compensation.
2. It was this deal that set him on _____ his first million.
3. From the seventh month onwards, with adequate care, a child born before full term has _____ survival.
4. If the two had been introduced simultaneously, the larger one would invariably have had _____.
5. Before he graduated as an MBA talent from the university, his parents had warned him that the journey of life had many _____.
6. People on lower incomes in that situation will suffer _____ those on higher incomes.
7. The government's dilemma is that sterling is falling because the financial markets no longer _____ government policy towards the pound.
8. Schools of choice have lower _____ rates, fewer discipline problems, better student attitudes, and higher teacher satisfaction.
9. The Congress Party in India lost its legislative majority in the late 1970s after nearly thirty years _____.
10. The two sisters had never needed each other more but weren't even speaking _____.

E. Read the following text and choose the best word for each blank from the choices given.

University students must attend a certain number of courses. In their first and second years, they usually (1) _____ courses in a wide range of subjects. In their third and fourth years, students may (2) _____ in their main subject. A (3) _____ course consists of three classes per week for one semester. A bachelor's degree (4) _____ about thirty-six courses, each lasting one semester. For every course they take, students are given a certain number of credits. When their credits amount (5) _____ the required number, they get a bachelor's degree. That's about four years' study at university. Higher degrees require (6) _____ study.

Because most American universities do not have entrance examinations, the first two years

Unit One

in a college or university are looked on as a (7) _____ period during which students must study a certain number of (8) _____ subjects and reach a certain scholastic level. If students (9) _____ to do so, they may be (10) _____ unless they find a way to repeat failed courses. In a big university, there (11) _____ be several thousand students taking a compulsory subject at the same time. They have to be divided into several (12) _____. This also makes it (13) _____ to employ closed-circuit and two-way television technology. Students (14) _____ know their professors well, since it is the teaching assistant who answers their questions and (15) _____ their exam papers.

1. A. take   B. receive   C. carry   D. recruit
2. A. attend   B. specialize   C. research   D. maintain
3. A. common   B. general   C. typical   D. average
4. A. requires   B. requests   C. studies   D. defines
5. A. up   B. to   C. in   D. at
6. A. more   B. better   C. further   D. harder
7. A. trial   B. test   C. check-in   D. basic
8. A. free   B. optional   C. compulsory   D. needed
9. A. get   B. like   C. permit   D. fail
10. A. recruited   B. dismissed   C. reset   D. discarded
11. A. must   B. could   C. may   D. will
12. A. rooms   B. discussions   C. campuses   D. classes
13. A. typical   B. desirable   C. unlikely   D. fundamental
14. A. seldom   B. often   C. generally   D. merely
15. A. reads   B. types   C. designs   D. marks

F. Translate the following sentences into English, using the phrases and expressions given in parentheses.

1. 这匹马在比赛进行一半时开始领先。(get ahead)
2. 如果她当时不替我说好话,公司不会录用我。(put a good word for)
3. 他伸出舌头,对着镜子仔细地看。(poke out)
4. 当房子倒塌的时候,人们惊恐地向后退。(draw back)
5. 街道上到处是垃圾。(be strewn with)
6. 丢失的包最后在湖边找到了,里面空空如也。(turn up)
7. 如果我丢了车钥匙就麻烦了。(be up the creek)
8. 这个问题本身不重要,但其长远影响可能很严重。(in itself)
9. 考虑到会下雨,他们关上了窗户。(in the expectation of)
10. 经过几年的努力,他终于感觉到走向成功了。(the road to)
11. 她的恢复堪比奇迹。(be little short of)
12. 在这个地区,警察在与毒贩的较量中占了上风。(have the upper hand)
13. 他想我们的关系得他说了算。(on one's own terms)

About Heroes

1. The word *hero* can be confusing, for it has several meanings. It is often applied to ordinary people who happen to perform an act of great courage—a fireman who saves someone from a burning house at the risk of his own life, for example. Then, the principal character of a play, a novel, or a film is known as the hero of the story, even if he is not particularly brave. But the heroes and heroines that we are going to consider now constitute a third group. They are the giants, the out-of-the-ordinary figures whose superiority fills our hearts with admiration and awe; the men and women who give us a high example to follow, a purpose in life, or sometimes just a dream, because they represent the person that we would like to be.

2. Humanity has always had such heroes. Some have been the saviors or the builders of their country, like **George Washington**①, who gave generations of Americans their model of determination, selflessness, and honor. Others have been religious leaders or gorgeous women; conquerors, athletes, or pioneers; characters in novels or revolutionaries; saints, sinners, likable robbers, or movie stars. Whatever they did, they were all stars—shining, glorious, showing the way to their followers below. The desire to be worthy of them could bring out the best in their admirers.

3. Many articles have appeared in recent years, claiming that there are no more heroes in the Western world. The authors say that, particularly in Europe and North America, the young now refuse to admire anyone; that we are living in a world too well informed, too curious and critical for hero worship. The press, books, and television keep showing us the faults of the public figures who could become today's stars, until we lose faith and start looking for defects in any person who seems worthy of respect. In a neighbor or a statesman, we try to discover the weaknesses, failures, or ugly motives that are surely hiding behind his noble actions.

4. Is it true that we know too much? Were our ancestors lucky to be only partly informed? Those who read the first biographies of **Charlemagne**②, George Washington, **Joan of Arc**③, or other great men and women of the past were not told that their hero had bad breath or disliked his mother; they only found a description of his great accomplishments and their admiration was strengthened. In fact, early biographers didn't hesitate to make up an admirable story or two about their hero. The man who wrote the first biography of Washington, for instance, invented the cherry tree; he admitted later that there was no truth in it, but he said that it was in character and that it would give young men a good example to follow. His readers didn't seem to object; the book was reprinted eighty times—a tremendous success in

those days.

5   Modern biographers do not invent such stories; they respect the facts, as indeed they should. But we pay a price for their truthfulness, for in their efforts to show "the whole person," they tell us more than we really need to know about private lives, family secrets, and human weaknesses. The true greatness of a fine man is often forgotten in the display; and people lose not only their admiration for him, but their willingness to trust any other "star" completely.

6   This shows clearly in the remarks of a group of high-school students near Los Angeles, who were asked whom they admired. "Nobody," said a young man, "because the objects of our early admiration have been destroyed. People we wanted to believe in have been described to us with all their faults and imperfections; that makes it hard to trust the 'historical' heroes." Another student, a girl, added, "The people we try to imitate are the unknown adults, the noncelebrities in our lives. Instead of dreaming of being like some famous woman somewhere, I want to be like my mom's best friend, whom no one in this room would know. But I know and admire her, and that's enough for me."

7   The qualities required of a hero vary with the times, and some great figures of a certain period would surprise the people of another generation. Consider the explosion of love and grief that followed the death of **John Lennon**[④] in December 1980. Few deaths have caused such deep sorrow, such mourning, in so many countries throughout the history of the world. There is no doubt that Lennon was a hero for his mourners. Why? What had he done that was so remarkable? "John was not just a musician," says one of his admirers. "He had known how to express my generation's feelings in the late 1960s. He was our voice and our guide; he changed with us over the years, always a little ahead of us; he opened new horizons for us and encouraged us to venture farther, to dare. To us he talked of love and peace; he was the big brother we needed in a troubled time." Some of Lennon's admirers may have been aware that he was not perfect; but they chose to ignore his dark side to remain grateful for the positive contribution he had made in their lives. There are surely many people who don't consider John Lennon a hero, who in fact have a very low opinion of him. But it is not unusual for one person's hero to be another person's villain. Think of all the leaders, revolutionaries, and conquerors who are deeply respected by one nation, one religious group, or one generation, and despised or hated by others.

8   Television and films offer many shallow heroes to their young audiences. Many parents are unhappy to see their children's admiration for Superman, Spiderman, or for some extravagant rock singer without ideas or talent. But such heroes do not last very long; and after a few years the growing teenagers are laughing at these objects of their young admiration. They start looking for better guides. And no matter what they say, they do find them. The student who was wise enough to recognize qualities in her mother has a perfectly good heroine of her own, and one who is much easier to imitate than George Washington or **Clara Barton**[⑤].

9   It may be difficult to be a hero in the Western world these days, under the searching

eyes of a critical society. But surely excellence has not disappeared completely; there are still individuals who are superior to their fellow men by their wisdom, their courage, or their character. They can be heroes if people are willing to ignore their human imperfections and to admit the respect that their admirable qualities inspire. Heroes are needed everywhere, at any time. It's a sad sky that has no shining stars.

Notes

① **George Washington** founder and first president of the United States (1732—1799). 乔治·华盛顿,美国第一任总统。

② **Charlemagne** Emperor of the West (742—814). 查理曼大帝。

③ **Joan of Arc** a French girl who fought for the liberation of her country, and was burned by the enemy at the age of nineteen (1412—1431).圣女贞德,法国民族英雄。

④ **John Lennon** an English singer, songwriter, musician, and activist who co-founded the Beatles, the most commercially successful and musically influential band in the history of popular music (1940—1980). 约翰·列侬,英国摇滚乐队"披头士"成员。

⑤ **Clara Barton** a pioneering nurse who founded the American Red Cross (1821—1912). 克拉丽莎·哈罗·巴顿,她创建了美国红十字会。

Exercises

Choose the correct answer to each of the following questions.

1. What kind of heroes does the author discuss?
   A. Common people with great courage.
   B. The principal character of a movie.
   C. Ordinary people with great fame.
   D. Exceptional figures.

2. What can heroes not do for their admirers?
   A. Bring out the best in them.
   B. Shed light on their way.
   C. Give them a purpose in life.
   D. Make them heroes.

3. According to recent articles, why has the Western world lost its admiration for heroes?
   A. People have become too critical.
   B. There are no more heroes.
   C. People are no longer curious.
   D. People don't need heroes any more.

4. What is the difference between early biographers and modern biographers?
   A. Early biographers didn't respect the facts.

B. Early biographers invented stories.

   C. Early biographers emphasized the great accomplishments of the heroes.

   D. Modern biographers pay more attention to human imperfections.

5. Why was John Lennon considered a great figure in his time?

   A. He was a great musician.

   B. He expressed his generation's feelings.

   C. He saved people's lives.

   D. He starred in many movies.

6. What is the author's opinion of "shallow heroes"?

   A. They are no great threat.

   B. They are better guides than parents.

   C. They last long.

   D. They have talents.

On-the-job Writing: Professional E-mail

E-mail is useful to many different kinds of businesses and organizations, but there is no one-size-fit-all format. Consequently, it's always a good idea to acquaint yourself with customary use of e-mail at your place of work. In addition, here are some suggestions for improving the quality of all electronic communication.

1. **Use a helpful subject line.** To ensure that your message will be opened and read, always use specific words in the subject line to clearly describe the central focus or key words of your correspondence.

2. **Begin appropriately.** A new communication should begin with an appropriate greeting, depending on the formality of the occasion. For example, if you are writing an officer of another company to ask for information, you might begin with a traditional salutation (Dear Mr. Hall). An informal memo to a coworker might have a more casual greeting, depending on your relationship to that person (Hello, Bill; Good morning, Ms. Merrill).

3. **Keep your message brief.** If possible, confine your message to one screen. Clearly state your purpose, explain in a concise manner, and conclude gracefully.

4. **Make it easy to read.** Keep your paragraph short, and skip lines between each paragraph. If your message is long, break it up with headings, numbered lists, or "bullets." Use a readable, plain font (字体,字号).

5. **Check your tone.** Your e-mail messages should sound professional and cordial. Unlike personal e-mail, which may contain slang, fragments, asides, or funny graphics, business e-mails should be written in good standard English and be straight to the point.

6. **Sign off.** If your e-mail is performing a task similar to that of a business letter, you may wish to close in a traditional way:

Yours truly,
Scott Muranjan

You may also want to create a standard sign-off that not only includes your name but also your title, telephone and fax number, mailing and e-mail address. Such information is helpful for readers who wish to contact you later.

However, if your e-mail is more akin to an informal memo between coworkers, you may find it appropriate to end with a friendly thought or word of thanks and your first name:

I'm looking forward to working with you on the Blue file. See you at Tuesday's meeting.
Scott

Allow your sense of the occasion and audience to dictate the kind of closing each e-mail requires.

SAMPLE EMAIL

From:	Ann Frost [Ann Frost@yahoo.com]
Sent:	Tuesday, November 7, 2017 10:34AM
To:	Maria London (Maria London@yahoo.com)
Subject:	Design for *Rules of Thumb*

Maria:

As I said on the phone, this is the cleanest, most attractive set of page designs we've ever seen. Many thanks for your care and creativity.

You have responded to nearly all of our issues. We have just a couple of remaining requests.

White Space
We would like more vertical space above subheadings. For example, page 10 of the layout sheets shows identical space above heads and paragraphs.

Titles and Headings
We particularly like the typefaces for the section titles and for subheadings. However page 37 is actually a new chapter; please change the headings and subheadings accordingly.

Thanks for your attention to our requests. For our part, we promise speedy responses during production.

Please call me if you have any questions.

Ann

Ann Frost
tel/fax 212.555.7039

Unit Two

Text A

Pre-reading Activities

1. You are going to read a story told by a son about his father who shapes the son's life in many ways. How can a father influence his son in life, work, and study?
2. The father could read and write nothing except his own name, yet he could be a good teacher and psychologist. How could that be?
3. The biggest dream of the father was to bring work and prosperity to his family and the people in the local town. How might he accomplish this?
4. What might the following words or expressions mean in the story?
   bless   who you are   what you do

Any More Like You at Home?
George Veazey

1   Though my father yearned to travel, he never managed in all of his 83 years to escape very far from Pecan Island. Pecan Island—that's our narrow strip of soil and trees separated from the **Louisiana**[①] mainland by miles of grass-covered tidal marsh. He was further shut off from the outside world by the fact that he couldn't read even the simplest newspaper headline and could write only two words—his name, Ulysse Veazey (pronounced vee-ZAY). He was constantly almost overwhelmed by the problems of trying to support a family of 20 on the often less than $350 a year he made from farming and trapping. (This family included 11 children of his own and the seven in-laws he took upon himself to raise.) Yet Papa refused to be hemmed in by circumstances, or to let us be.

2   We Louisiana **Cajuns**[②] are often called "Webfeet" because we can get around in the marshes and bayous about as easily as ducks. I must have been about seven when I first heard that nickname. It was jeered at me by some older boys, who had come to Pecan Island by mail boat from the nearest small town, Abbeville, 50 miles away. They were too big to fight, and I ran home furious, on the verge of tears.

3   "Stop that sniveling and come with me," Papa said sternly. Then, for the first time, he took me on one of his trapping rounds in the swamp. Tall and husky with curly, crow-black hair and dark, no-nonsense eyes, he seemed to me a giant as he effortlessly poled his pirogue

along. We hadn't gone far before the high marsh grass closed around us, curtaining off familiar landmarks. Suddenly, every one of the countless, tea-dark water passages looked alarmingly alike to me.

4 "Think you could find your way home from here?" Papa asked.

5 "No, sir, I'm lost."

6 "Well, I'm not," he said, eyes twinkling, "because I'm a Webfoot—and you'd better be glad of that. Because if I weren't, neither one of us would ever find our way out of this swamp!" His voice grew serious again: "Son, never be ashamed of who or what you are." From that moment on, I was proud of being a Webfoot.

A Lesson to Remember

7 If my father ever resented his hard lot or felt the least twinge of self-pity, he never showed it. Instead, he liked to remember the progress he had made. With his own hands, Papa had built our plain but impressive two-story house in a grove of wild pecan trees and live oaks on the highest rise on the island. The house he had grown up in as a boy, he liked to remind us, had had a dirt floor, no panes in the windows, and no lighting but candles. Ours had a good wood floor, windows with glass in them, and kerosene lanterns.

8 For one who had never sat in a classroom, my father was quite a teacher. Take, for instance, what happened during my Christmas holidays when I was 11. On the night my vacation began, Papa inquired, "Son, how're you doing with your sixth-grade work?"

9 "Oh, so-so, I guess."

10 "That's what I thought," was all he said then. But next morning, at daybreak, he took me out to help him dig a new canal. (In most of the marsh, the grass is so thick that you cannot pole a pirogue through it except via a canal.) We stood knee-deep in numbing winter water and dug up shovelfuls of grass and mud, making a passageway about 3 and a half feet wide and 18 inches deep. We dug from dawn to sunset for the rest of my two-week vacation and lengthened that canal by half a mile. When, at the end of the last day, I flopped into the pirogue exhausted, Papa put his hand on my shoulder. "*Vieux Tronc* (Old Stump), you're tired, aren't you?"

11 "Yes, sir," I blurted angrily, "I'm tired and I'm cold."

12 "Well, I'm tired and cold, too. Son, you don't like digging much, do you?"

13 "No, sir, I hate it!"

14 "Of course you do," Papa said. "And that's what I want you to remember when you go back to your studying. Because I never went to school, this kind of work is all I can do: feed the stock, milk the cows, plow, hunt, trap, and dig this canal. If you don't do good in school, you can look forward to another 50 years of this kind of work."

15 A harsh way to drive home a lesson? Maybe. But I never forgot it. After that, my schoolwork picked up considerably.

Friendly Persuasion

16 A warm understanding of human nature not to be learned from books made my father a good psychologist. A few years before I was born, Papa and other lay leaders had raised enough money to complete Pecan Island's first **Catholic church**[3]; but they still lacked $90 to add the final touch—the bell in the steeple. Papa tried to get a donation from old Chapie Marceau, a well-to-do rancher and friend of the family. Chapie, who said he didn't believe in church, hotly refused.

17 Papa just smiled and seemed to drop the matter. Even when he went to spend a weekend with Chapie, he made a point of not mentioning it—until, at the supper table the first night, the old man blurted out, "Ulysse, I am no fool. I know why you're here, and you're wasting your time. I won't give you $90—or even 90 cents—for no church bell!"

18 "Oh, forget about that," Papa said soothingly. "We can find plenty of old men who'll be glad to give the money. The only reason I asked you was out of respect; I think of you as my godfather. You see, Parrin (Godfather) Chapie, you are one of the elders of our parish. What could have been more fitting than for you, who adore children, to have given the bell? Every Sunday morning, the little children all over the island would have heard that bell ringing, and they would have said, 'Listen, Parrin Chap's calling us to church now. He's calling us to worship and do something good today.' So they would have all remembered you—not for a day, or a year, but as long as the generations heard that bell ringing. But you didn't want that, so I suppose our children and grandchildren will have to listen to somebody else's bell ring."

19 Old Chapie glared fiercely and, without a word, got up and went to bed. But, the next morning at breakfast, he said: "Ulysse, tell me that story again about how the little children will come to church every Sunday—and about how they're going to remember me by that bell I'm going to give them." And that's why to this day the Chapie Marceau Bell still chimes on Pecan Island.

Impossible High School

20 I thought I'd have to quit school after the tenth grade, for that was as far as our crude three-room school on the island went. Only one of my five older brothers and sisters had finished high school. He did it by going somewhere else to live. By the time I was 14, we were in the depths of the **Depression**[4]. There didn't seem to be a chance for us six younger Veazeys to get high school diplomas.

21 Then Papa, who had been quietly simmering over the situation for years, decided to take action. He put on his "best suit"—his newest pair of overalls—and went before the school board in Abbeville and asked them to give Pecan Island an accredited high school. The board chairman told him, of course, that that was impossible. "We'd need extra taxes," he explained, "and the great majority of voters in our district live on the mainland. They'd never agree to a tax increase to provide an out-of-the-way school that would serve so few

students."

22 Papa didn't believe it; he thought more of people than that, he said. So, he got on a mule and rode from house to house all over the mainland part of the district. His approach was anything but subtle. "Mr. LeBlanc," he said, "you can send your child to high school in Abbeville. I can't. Now, Mr. LeBlanc, you're my neighbor, and a fair one, I know. So, please sign this paper saying you'll favor more taxes to give my children the same chance in life that yours have."

23 Put like that, it was hard to say no. Nearly everyone signed the petition, and we got our "impossible" high school.

A Plea for Progress

24 Years ahead of our neighbors in some ways, Papa was the first to fight for a road to Pecan Island. He even borrowed a high-wheeled marsh buggy and personally surveyed a line to Little Prairie, where he thought the first link of the road should run. He talked up the idea to **governors**[5] **and senators** who came to hunt with him. "You wouldn't be building it just for a handful of islanders," he pointed out. "A highway through here to Port Arthur could cut 50 miles off the drive from **New Orleans** to **Texas**."

25 His urging grew more insistent when one of his small grandsons, stricken with diphtheria, died in his arms on the 12-hour mail-boat trip to the doctor in Abbeville. When, ten years later, my sister Mayvel lost twin sons in childbirth on the same voyage, Papa became almost fanatical in his pleas for the road. Finally, in 1952, it was built. On our first drive over the highway from Abbeville, Papa looked as proud as if he had laid every foot of it himself.

26 In the summer of 1940 the Union Oil Company struck a gusher four miles north of our house. My father agreed to lease his land to the company, and he urged our suspicious neighbors to lease theirs. In thanks, the company asked, "What can we do for you?"

27 "You can give our boys here the same chance at jobs that you're giving outsiders you're bringing in from **California**, Texas, and **Oklahoma**," Papa said. "A chance to start at the bottom is all I ask for them."

28 My cousin and I, the first islanders given the opportunity to try out as roustabouts, were plenty nervous as we set forth from home that first morning, and Papa gave us a pep talk. "Sure, you'll be competing against veterans who know their stuff," he said. "But remember, they're not used to the marsh. They're not Webfeet—you are!"

29 Staggering through the muck beneath loads of timbers and pipe joints was rough on us, but a lot rougher on the workers from outside. Within a week, most of them had quit. The manager called in my cousin and me, and asked, "You got any more Webfeet like you at home?" We did, and that started the fulfillment of Papa's biggest dream—work and prosperity for the people on Pecan Island.

"We've Been Blessed"

30 Mama died in 1962, and Papa turned to the marsh for comfort, to the solace of its silent vastness and the oneness he felt with nature there. He hunted and trapped until after he was 80. Then, when he could no longer handle the boat, he gardened. At 83, becoming even too weak for that, he just sat quietly in the big chair in his room and thought and rocked.

31 He was sitting there the last time I ever saw him alive, on a July evening in 1967. "Son," he said feebly, "come and sit a while. I want to talk to you." We talked a long time about the good days and bad we'd had together. We talked about how pewter-gray but grand the marsh was in winter with **the Vs of ducks and geese**⑥ swinging downwind and how different and soft it was with the blanket of blue irises covering it in the spring.

32 Finally, he turned and looked out the window toward the sun going down. "Old Stump," he said, "in a few hours I'm going to be dead." He waved aside my protests. "Yes," he said, "I guess I'm as ready as anybody ever gets. We've been blessed, your mama and me—nine of you children still living, and 48 grandchildren and great-grand-children—and most of 'em, I guess, will be going to college. Think of that."

33 His voice dropped almost to a whisper. "Strange," he said, eyes clouding with troubled wonder, as if what he was about to say had just occurred to him. "Strange, I can't take one dollar with me, or a single cow, or even a grain of sand." He slumped down, and I thought that was all.

34 But I should have known that Papa always ended any good talk on a strong note. Rousing again, he said, with something like his old authority, "Listen, son, I'm leaving all of you a few dollars in the bank and a few acres of land, and I don't want any of you fussing or bickering over little things like that. I want you to be the kind of brothers and sisters we raised you to be. And remember that each time you have a meeting of the family, your mother and I will be sitting at that meeting with you. You see," he said, brightening considerably, "we're really not leaving you at all. No, we'll be staying right here, watching and listening and being proud of you and..." His voice trailed off, and this time didn't come back.

35 Papa just never could stop being head of the family, and that's what he'll always be, even though he watches over us now from an empty chair.

Notes

① **Louisiana**   state in the south central United States, bordering on the Gulf of Mexico, （美国）路易斯安那州

Texas   south central state bordering on the Gulf of Mexico and Mexico, （美国）得克萨斯州

California   western state, extending along the Pacific Ocean, (美国)加利福尼亚州

Oklahoma   south central state, north of Texas, (美国)俄克拉荷马州

Unit Two

New Orleans   large Louisiana city, located on the Mississippi River delta, 新奥尔良市(位于路易斯安那州)

Port Arthur   port city on the Texas/Louisiana border, 亚瑟港市(位于得克萨斯州)

② **Cajun**   somebody from Louisiana who is descended from French colonists exiled in the eighteenth century from Acadia in present-day Canada, 他们的祖先(2500 到 3000 人)于 1764 到 1788 年间从阿卡迪亚地区流落到路易斯安那地区(均为前法国殖民地)

③ **Catholic Church**   church that regards itself as continuing the traditions of the Christian church before Christianity became divided into Catholicism and Protestantism in the Protestant Reformation, 天主教(的)

④ **the Depression**   Great Depression in the United States, worst and longest economic collapse in the history of the modern industrial world, lasting from the end of 1929 until the early 1940s, 美国经济大萧条时期

⑤ **governor**   the elected executive of state-level government in the United States, (美国)州长

senator   an elected or appointed member of a senate. In the United States, the Senate is one of the two legislative bodies in the national government or in state governments, (美国)参议员

⑥ **the Vs of ducks and geese**   V-shaped formation of ducks and geese in flight, 野鸭和大雁的 V 字队形

Vocabulary

1. yearn [jɜːn] *vt.* to long for; to have a strong desire for somebody or something, especially when the desire is tinged with sadness, 渴望,期望
2. marsh [mɑːʃ] *n.* soft wet ground, an area of low-lying waterlogged land, often beside water, that is poorly drained and liable to flood, difficult to cross on foot, and unfit for agriculture or building, 沼泽地
3. overwhelm [əʊvəˈwelm] *vt.* (*often passive*) to overpower somebody emotionally or physically; to provide somebody with a huge amount; to surge over somebody or something, 使陷入某种情绪;压倒,制服
4. hem [hem] *v.* to surround and enclose somebody or something, 包围,限制,约束
5. webfoot [ˈwebfʊt] *n.* foot with toes joined by webbing, 带有蹼的脚
6. bayou [ˈbaɪuː] *n.* marshland; in the southern United States, an area of slow-moving water, often overgrown with reeds, leading from a river or lake, 美国南部的长沼
7. jeer [dʒɪə] *v.* to express derision vocally, to shout or laugh at somebody or something in a mocking or scornful way, 嘲笑,嘲弄
8. furious [ˈfjʊərɪəs] *adj.* infuriated, extremely or violently angry, 满腔愤怒的,大发雷霆的
9. snivel [ˈsnɪv(ə)l] *vi.* to whine, to behave in a whining, tearful, or self-pitying way, 伤心地啼哭或抽泣

10. stern [stɜːn] *adj.* strict, rigid, and uncompromising; forbidding, grim, austere in appearance, 严厉的, 苛刻的, 不苟言笑的

11. swamp [swɒmp] *n.* wetland, an area of land, usually fairly large, that is always wet and is overgrown with various shrubs and trees, 湿地

12. husky [ˈhʌskɪ] *adj.* burly and compact in physique, solid, burly, compact, 高大, 强壮, 魁梧; throaty, hoarse and dry, either naturally or as a result of illness or emotion, 喉咙发干, 沙哑

13. pole [pəʊl] *v.* to move a boat along by pushing with a pole against a firm surface, 用杆撑船

14. pirogue [pɪˈrəʊg] *n.* dugout canoe, a canoe made from a hollowed-out tree trunk, used especially in southern Louisiana, 路易丝安那州南部常见的一种用掏空的树干做成的小船

15. landmark [ˈlæn(d)mɑːk] *n.* a prominent structure or geographic feature that identifies a location and serves as a guide to finding it; boundary marker, a conspicuous object, e.g., a tree or stone, that is recognized as marking the boundary of a piece of land, 地标, 界标

16. twinkle [ˈtwɪŋk(ə)l] *vi.* to shine with flicker, to give out or reflect a bright but unsteady light, especially from a small or distant source; to shine with amusement, to be bright because of a feeling such as amusement, delight, or mischief (*refers to people's eyes*), 闪烁, 闪耀, (眼睛)发亮, 闪光

17. resent [rɪˈzent] *vt.* be annoyed at, to feel aggrieved about something or toward somebody, often because of a perceived wrong or injustice, 感到愤恨、怨恨或气愤

18. twinge [twɪn(d)ʒ] *n.* a sudden brief stab of pain; a sudden brief uncomfortable pang of an emotion such as guilt or fear, 阵痛, 刺痛

19. plain [pleɪn] *adj.* simple and ordinary, without ornamentation or frills; not attractive, not pretty or good-looking, 简朴的, 普通的, 毫无装饰的

20. grove [grəʊv] *n.* group of trees; orchard, 树丛, 小树林

21. pecan [ˈpɪˈkæn] *n.* a large hickory tree that has deeply furrowed bark and produces pecans, native to the southern United States and Mexico, 美州山核桃树

22. oak [əʊk] *n.* a deciduous or evergreen tree with acorns as fruit and leaves with several rounded or pointed lobes, grown for its shade and wood, native to the northern hemisphere, 橡树

23. rise [raɪz] *n.* upward slope, an upward slope or gradient; higher ground, a hill or piece of raised or rising ground, 高坡, 高地

24. pane [peɪn] *n.* glazed section of window, a piece of glass in a window frame, 窗户上的玻璃

25. kerosene/kerosine [ˈkɛrəˌsɪn] *n.* a colorless flammable oil distilled from petroleum, used as fuel for jet engines, heating, cooking, and lighting, 煤油

26. daybreak [ˈdeɪbreɪk] *n.* dawn, the time when light first appears in the sky at the beginning of a day, 黎明

27. canal [kəˈnæl] *n.* an artificial waterway constructed for shipping, irrigation, or recreational use, (人工挖凿的)运河

28. via [ˈvaɪə] *prep.* through, by way of or through, 经由; by means of, using the means or agency of, 通过

29. numbing ['nʌmɪŋ] *adj.* causing numbness, deadening feelings or thoughts; temporarily taking away somebody's ability to feel or think, 使失去知觉的,使麻木的

30. shovel ['ʃʌv(ə)l] *n.* long-handled scoop, a hand tool consisting of a broad, usually curved blade attached to a long handle, used for lifting and moving loose material, 铁锹

31. flop [flɒp] *vi.* to sit or lie down heavily by relaxing the muscles and letting the body fall, 重重地坐下或躺下

32. blurt [blɜːt] *vt.* say something impulsively, to say something suddenly or impulsively, as if by accident, 脱口说出

33. lay [leɪ] *adj.* not belonging to clergy, belonging to or involving the people of a church who are not members of the clergy; untrained, without expertise or professional training in a specific field, 非神职的,非专业的,外行的

34. steeple ['stiːp(ə)l] *n.* a tower forming part of a Christian church or another building, usually with a spire on top, 教堂的尖顶

35. rancher ['rɑːn(t)ʃə] *n.* someone who owns or manages a ranch or large cattle/sheep farm with extensive areas for grazing, 牧场主

36. hotly ['hɒtlɪ] *adv.* angrily, in an angry way; fiercely, in an intense and committed way, 愤怒地,热烈地,激烈地,坚决地

37. soothe [suːð] *v.* to ease pain, to make pain or discomfort less severe; calm somebody down, to make somebody less angry, anxious, or upset, 缓解(疼痛);平静或镇定,安慰,抚慰

38. parish ['pærɪʃ] *n.* district with its own church, in the Episcopal, Roman Catholic, and some other churches, 教区,牧区

39. adore [ə'dɔː] *vt.* to love somebody deeply; to like something very much, 喜爱,热爱,崇敬

40. worship ['wɜːʃɪp] *v.* to treat somebody or something as divine and show respect by engaging in acts of prayer and devotion; to take part in a religious service; to love, admire, or respect somebody or something greatly and perhaps excessively or unquestioningly, 崇拜;做礼拜;爱慕

41. glare [gleə] *v.* to stare stonily, to stare intently and angrily, 怒目而视; to express something with a stare, to express or signal anger, disapproval, contempt, or another negative emotion by giving a steady stare, 用愤怒的目光表达

42. fierce [fɪəs] *adj.* aggressive, violent or intense, 凶狠的,强烈的,激烈的

43. chime [tʃaɪm] *v.* to ring melodiously, (钟)响,敲出乐声

44. crude [kruːd] *adj.* not well finished, not completely worked out, rough, 粗陋的,简陋的

45. diploma [dɪ'pləʊmə] *n.* course certificate, a certificate given by a high school, college, university, or professional organization indicating that one has completed a course of education or training and reached the required level of competence,(毕业)证书,文凭

46. simmer ['sɪmə] *v.* to cook something gently just below the boiling point, usually with the occasional bubble breaking on the surface; to have anger or another strong emotion building up inside, often without being expressed, 煨,炖;憋着,按捺着

47. overall ['əʊvərɔːl] *n.* protective garment, a loose-fitting lightweight piece of clothing like a coat or loose pants, sometimes worn over ordinary clothes to protect them, 长罩衣

48. accredit [əˈkredɪt] vt. to officially recognize a person or thing, validate, 给予官方认可
49. mule [mjuːl] n. the offspring of a female horse and a male donkey, 毛驴
50. petition [pɪˈtɪʃ(ə)n] n. a written request signed by many people demanding a specific action from an authority or government, 请愿书
51. buggy [ˈbʌgɪ] n. a lightweight horse-drawn carriage; a small battery-powered vehicle used for a particular purpose; a lightweight baby carriage, 轻便马车, 电瓶车, 婴儿车
52. diphtheria [dɪfˈθɪərɪə; dɪp-] n. infectious disease causing constriction of the throat, 白喉
53. fanatical [fəˈnætɪkəl] adj. excessively enthusiastic about a particular belief, cause, or activity, 狂热的
54. plea [pliː] n. an urgent, often emotional, request, 恳求, 请求
55. voyage [ˈvɒɪɪdʒ] n. long trip, a long journey, especially one by sea or through space, (航海、航空)航行
56. gusher [ˈgʌʃə] n. free-flowing oil well, 喷油井
57. lease [liːs] vt. to rent property to somebody or from somebody, 出租或租得
58. veteran [ˈvet(ə)r(ə)n] n. somebody formerly in the armed forces, experienced soldier; somebody with experience, 退伍老兵, 老军人, 有丰富经验的人, 老手
59. timber [ˈtɪmbə] n. standing trees or their wood, especially when suitable for sawing into building materials, 用材林; 木材, 木料
60. rough [rʌf] adj. severe or unpleasant, unfair, 不愉快的, 不幸的
61. solace [ˈsɒlɪs] n. relief from emotional distress, a source of comfort, 安慰, 慰藉; 给予安慰的事物
62. rock [rɒk] v. to sway to and fro, (前后或左右)摆动, 摇晃
63. feeble [ˈfiːb(ə)l] adj. physically or mentally weak; unconvincing, 虚弱的, 微弱的, 衰弱的; 无力的
64. iris [ˈaɪrɪs] n. flowering plant with long sword-shaped leaves and multi-colored flowers, 鸢尾属植物
65. slump [slʌmp] vi. to collapse, to sink or fall suddenly and heavily, 沉重地落下或倒下
66. fuss [fʌs] vi. to be too concerned about details or trivial matters, (为小事)烦恼、激动
67. bicker [ˈbɪkə] vi. to argue in a bad-tempered way about something unimportant, (为小事)争吵

Useful Expressions

1. **shut off**: to isolate, separate
   (1) The village was shut off by mountains from the rest of the world, yet many young villagers still dreamed of going beyond the mountains to the outside world one day.
   (2) Living in the countryside has shut him off from city life.
2. **take upon oneself**: to assume as a responsibility or obligation
   (1) As a teacher, she takes it upon herself to help the students with their homework after class.
   (2) One mustn't take upon oneself the right to make every decision for the committee.

3. **hem in :** to enclose or confine
   (1) The enemies were hemming our troops in.
   (2) I always felt hemmed in by conventions.
4. **curtain off:** to separate or divide by means of a curtain or curtains
   (1) One corner of the room was curtained off as a wardrobe.
   (2) A tall building was erected in front of our house, curtaining off the mountain view from us.
5. **well-to-do:** having more than adequate financial resources
   (1) They looked like a group of well-to-do tourists, purchasing all sorts of souvenirs wherever they went.
   (2) Students from well-to-do families were shocked by what they saw in poverty-stricken areas.
6. **know one's stuff:** to be competent or well-informed, especially in a particular field; to be knowledgeable
   (1) His colleagues see him as a gifted teacher who knows his stuff.
   (2) What I expected of her was nothing more than knowing her stuff.
7. **pep talk:** a talk intended to fill the listeners with an urge to complete something well
   (1) Before I stepped onto the stage, my parents gave me a pep talk.
   (2) It is typical of the manager to excite his staff with a pep talk first thing in the morning.
8. **trail off:** to become gradually weaker and fade away
   (1) His interest in work has never trailed off, which is really admirable.
   (2) The baby cried sleepily in his mother's arms, his voice trailing off before he fell asleep.
9. **grow up:** to be or become fully grown, to attain maturity
   (1) He grew up listening to country music.
   (2) What are you going to do when you grow up?
10. **for instance:** as an example, for example
    (1) His spelling is terrible! For instance, look at this word!
    (2) There was something strange about James; for instance, he could not speak.
11. **look forward to:** to expect, to look into the future with expectation
    (1) Christmas is coming—children are looking forward to a pleasant holiday with lots of gifts from their parents.
    (2) If you don't finish the work today, you can look forward to another difficult day.
12. **pick up:** to make progress, improve
    (1) Sooner or later our production will pick up if we continue working hard.
    (2) We've been through some difficult times, but things will be picking up soon.
13. **make a point of:** to do something because one feels it necessary or important
    (1) I always make a point of checking spelling and grammar before I hand in my English papers.
    (2) We make a point of being punctual whenever we attend an activity.

14. **make it:** *informal* to succeed, to achieve success

    (1) He's really made it as an athlete.

    (2) Now we are on the top of the mountain. We made it.

15. **talk up:** to promote with enthusiasm, to make appear more important

    (1) At the meeting, Tom talked up the idea of giving more rights to the students.

    (2) He will use the chance of hosting a television program to talk up his latest book.

16. **try out:** to compete for a position or a role by taking part in a trial or test

    (1) Nancy tried out for the leading role in the play.

    (2) You can't join the team if you don't try out.

17. **call in:** to ask for help with a difficult situation

    (1) The government called in troops to stop the disturbances.

    (2) It is too late to call in a technician to fix your computer at this time.

18. **set forth:** to start on a journey; to make known

    (1) When will you set forth on your trip to the mountains?

    (2) The President set forth the aims of government in a television broadcast.

19. **anything but:** definitely not

    (1) The hotel was anything but satisfactory.

    (2) The joke he told was anything but funny.

20. **occur to:** to come into one's mind

    (1) It just occurred to me that he might know how to find her.

    (2) It never occurred to her to ask anyone.

Understanding the Text

1. How did the author manage to show that his father was not limited by circumstances?
2. What lesson did his father drive home when he took his son out to dig a canal?
3. What aspect of human nature do you see when Chapie Marceau was finally persuaded by the father to donate money for the church bell?
4. How did the impossible high school become possible? What was the less-than-subtle approach of the father?
5. What progress did the father help to make for the islanders?
6. Before the father died, he said that his life had been blessed. In what way had his life been blessed?
7. What character qualities do you see in the father? How would you describe the relationship between father and son?
8. How do you understand the title?

Unit Two

Exercises

A. Fill in the blanks with the appropriate words from the text.

1. Though my father _____ to travel, he never managed in all of his life to escape very far from the local town. He was further _____ from the outside world. He was constantly _____ by the problem of trying to support a family of twenty _____ the often less than $350 a year he made from farming and trapping.
2. For one who had never sat in a classroom, my father was _____ a teacher, and _____ of human nature not to be learned from books made my father a good psychologist.
3. The son thought he would have to quit school after the tenth grade, for that was _____ their crude three-room school went.
4. After the father asked the son to help dig the canal in the cold winter water, he said to him, "_____."

B. Choose from the words given below to complete the following sentences, changing the word form where necessary.

overwhelm	sternly	yearn	raise
resent	solace	serious	subtle
quite	authority	impressive	prosperity

1. He has been living in a foreign country for several years, but recently he found himself _____ by a feeling of homesickness.
2. Tom volunteered to work as an English teacher in the small town, but he _____ being used to make money for somebody else.
3. Nobody would deny that work and _____ were the scope of our parents' lives.
4. The reason some people keep pets is that those lovely animals are great _____ to them.
5. Sam _____ to be a policeman from an early age, but he changed his mind when he grew up.
6. The two paintings are similar to each other, but there are _____ differences between them.
7. We had a reunion party celebrating the twentieth anniversary of our graduation from university. It was _____ an occasion.
8. The work was exhausting: _____ funds, managing people and institutions.
9. "Something's bothering you, isn't it?" she said, her face now _____.
10. "Now get a move on, and that's an order," the matron said _____.

C. Fill in the blanks with the phrases given below, changing the form where necessary.

make it	pick up	jeer at
hem in	make a point of	get around
for instance	talk up	take upon oneself
look forward to	shut off	call in
take action	get up	set forth

1. What is most important at this point is _____ the new idea to the manager so that something can be done against the sales slide.
2. Don't worry, once he comes to the States, his English will _____ quickly.
3. With the Internet and modern communication technology, it is almost impossible for one person _____ from the rest of the world, even if he is in a far and remote place.
4. It is a good habit _____ closing the windows and doors before leaving the office.
5. These days, it is very common for the husband _____ it _____ to do housework, as more and more married women go out to work.
6. In spite of trying very hard, he _____ never really _____ as an actor.
7. Although born into a poor family, Tom has refused _____ by fate or circumstances.
8. If we miss this chance for economic development, we may _____ another fifty years of social and economic stagnation.
9. Don't mind how much it will cost. Just _____ him _____ if he can help us to solve the problem.
10. They were about to _____ on a voyage into the unknown.

D. Fill in the blanks with the expressions given below, changing the form where necessary.

on the verge of	in the depths of	ahead of
hard lot	anything but	a pep talk
well-to-do	a touch	in thanks
on a strong note	out-of-the-way	at the bottom of

1. The country is _____ collapse after being involved in a ten-year-long civil war.
2. Father was born into a poor working class family, but he never gave in to his _____.
3. Even _____ the turbulent times the young man would spend every minute on study and eventually turned out to be an excellent scholar in classical languages.
4. The visit to Paris was _____ success. Almost everybody lost something, either money or bags.
5. I was surprised to find the politician did not finish his talk _____, which was in fact his usual style of speaking.
6. _____ is something that could encourage people and lead them to take a positive attitude toward work and study.
7. Is it necessary that _____ people give large donations when natural disasters take place?

Unit Two

8. The manager of the company acknowledged _____ the contribution of all the staff.
9. Looking thin but not ill and oozing confidence but not cockiness, Victoria Beckham added _____ of spice to London Fashion Week.
10. A return label is provided for your convenience _____ the form.

E. Read the following text and choose the best word for each blank from the choices given.

The men methodically prepared for the hurricane. Since water power might be damaged, they filled bathtubs and pails. A power (1) _____ was likely, so they checked out batteries for the portable radio and flashlights, and fuel for the lantern. John's father moved a small generator into the downstairs hallway, wired several light bulbs to it and prepared a connection (2) _____ the refrigerator.

Rain fell (3) _____ that afternoon; gray clouds moved in from the Gulf on the rising wind. The family had an early supper. A neighbor, (4) _____ husband was in Vietnam, asked if she and her two children could sit (5) _____ the storm with the Koshas. Another neighbor came (6) _____ on his way inland—would the Koshas (7) _____ taking care of his dog?

It grew dark before seven o'clock. Wind and rain now whipped the house. John sent his oldest son and daughter upstairs to bring down mattresses and pillows for the children. He wanted to keep the group together on one floor. "Stay away from the windows," he warned, (8) _____ about glass flying from storm-shattered panes. As the wind (9) _____ to roar, the house began leaking—the rain seemingly (10) _____ right through the walls. With mops, towels, pots and buckets the Koshas began a struggle against the rapidly spreading water.

1. A. surplus   B. damage   C. outage   D. scarcity
2. A. to   B. in   C. at   D. for
3. A. steadily   B. seriously   C. largely   D. consistently
4. A. her   B. which   C. whose   D. that
5. A. out   B. in   C. down   D. with
6. A. by   B. in   C. out   D. down
7. A. care   B. mind   C. be   D. like
8. A. told   B. concerned   C. thought   D. complained
9. A. became   B. climbed   C. mounted   D. ceased
10. A. driven   B. forced   C. motivated   D. moved

F. Translate the following sentences into English, using the phrases and expressions given in parentheses.

1. 节假日里少了平时的压力,这让人感到很舒服。(shut off)
2. 这些志愿者们承担了让这些乡村孩子受教育的责任。(take sth upon oneself)
3. 他们用各种各样的规则和禁令来约束孩子。(hem in)
4. 我儿子说长大以后要当一名篮球教练。(grow up)
5. 如果我们今年不按时完成任务,明年又会很辛苦。(look forward to)

6. 经过一番训练,孩子们的英语水平提高得很快。(pick up)
7. 为了能提高成绩,他决定要花足够的时间来学习。(make a point of)
8. 成功当然让人高兴,不费很大劲就获得成功更让人敬佩。(make it)
9. 关键的问题是要在会上向领导们宣传这个好主意。(talk up)
10. 你只有试一试后才能知道能否入队。(try out)

Text B

Only Daughter
Sandra Cisneros

1   Once, several years ago, when I was just starting out in my writing career, I was asked to write my own contributor's note for an anthology. I wrote: "I am the only daughter in a family of six sons. That explains everything."

2   Well, I've thought about that ever since, and yes, it explains a lot to me, but for the reader's sake I should have written: "I am the only daughter in a *Mexican* family of six sons." Or even: "I am the only daughter of a Mexican father and a Mexican-American mother." Or: "I am the only daughter in a working-class family of nine." All of these had everything to do with who I am today.

3   I was/am the only daughter and *only* a daughter. Being an only daughter in a family of six sons forced me by circumstance to spend a lot of time by myself because my brothers felt it beneath them to play with a *girl* in public. But that aloneness, that loneliness, was good for a would-be writer—it allowed me time to think and think, to imagine, to read and prepare myself. Being only a daughter for my father meant my destiny would lead me to become someone's wife. That's what he believed. But when I was in the fifth grade and shared my plans for college with him, I was sure he understood. I remember my father saying, "*Que bueno, mi'ja,* that's good." That meant a lot to me, especially since my brothers thought the idea hilarious. What I didn't realize was that my father thought college was good for girls—good for finding a husband. After four years in college and two more in graduate school, and still no husband, my father shakes his head even now and says I wasted all that education.

4   In retrospect, I'm lucky my father believed daughters were meant for husbands. It meant it didn't matter if I majored in something silly like English. After all, I'd find a nice profession eventually, right? This allowed me the liberty to putter about embroidering my little poems and stories without my father interrupting with so much as a "What's that you're writing?"

5   But the truth is, I wanted him to interrupt. I wanted my father to understand what it was I was scribbling, to introduce me as "My only daughter, the writer." Not as "This is my only

daughter. She teaches." ***Es maestro***①—teacher. Not even ***profesora***②.

6   In a sense, everything I have ever written has been for him, to win his approval, even though I know my father can't read English words, even though my father's only reading includes the brown-ink *Esto* sports magazines from Mexico City and the bloody ***Alarma***③! magazines that feature yet another sighting of **La Virgen de Guadalupe**④ on a tortilla or a wife's revenge on her philandering husband by bashing his skull in with a *molcajete* (a kitchen mortar made of volcanic rock). Or the ***fotonovelas***⑤, the little picture paperbacks with tragedy and trauma erupting from the characters' mouths in bubbles.

7   A father represents, then, the public majority. A public who is disinterested in reading, and yet one whom I am writing about and for, and privately trying to woo.

8   When we were growing up in Chicago, we moved a lot because of my father. He suffered bouts of nostalgia. Then we'd have to let go of our flat, store the furniture with mother's relatives, load the station wagon with baggage and bologna sandwiches and head south. To Mexico City.

9   We came back, of course. To yet another Chicago flat, another Chicago neighborhood, another Catholic school. Each time, my father would seek out the parish priest in order to get a tuition break and complain or boast: "I have seven sons."

10   He meant *siete hijos*, seven children, but he translated it as "sons." "I have seven sons." To anyone who would listen. The Sears Roebuck employee who sold us the washing machine. The short-order cook where my father ate his ham-and-eggs breakfasts. "I have seven sons." As if he deserved a medal from the state.

11   My papa. He didn't mean anything by that mistranslation, I'm sure. But somehow I could feel myself being erased. I'd tug my father's sleeve and whisper: "Not seven sons. Six! and *one daughter*."

12   When my oldest brother graduated from medical school, he fulfilled my father's dream that we study hard and use this—our heads, instead of this—our hands. Even now my father's hands are thick and yellow, stubbed by a history of hammer and nails and twine and coils and springs. "Use this," my father said, tapping his head, "and not this," showing us those hands. He always looked tired when he said it.

13   Wasn't college an investment? And hadn't I spent all those years in college? And if I didn't marry, what was it all for? Why would anyone go to college and then choose to be poor? Especially someone who had always been poor.

14   Last year, after ten years of writing professionally, the financial rewards started to trickle in. My second **National Endowment for the Arts Fellowship**⑥. A guest professorship at **the University of California, Berkeley**⑦. My book, which sold to a major New York publishing house.

15   At Christmas, I flew home to Chicago. The house was throbbing, same as always; hot ***tamales***⑧ and sweet *tamales* hissing in my mother's pressure cooker, and everybody— my mother, six brothers, wives, babies, aunts, cousins—talking too loud and at the same time,

16   I went upstairs to my father's room... One of my stories had just been translated into Spanish and published in an anthology of Chicano writing, and I wanted to show it to him. Ever since he recovered from a stroke two years ago, my father likes to spend his leisure hours horizontally. And that's how I found him, watching a **Pedro Infante**⑨ movie on **Galavision**⑩ and eating rice pudding.

17   There was a glass filmed with milk on the bedside table. There were several vials of pills and balled **Kleenex**⑪. And on the floor, one black sock and a plastic urinal that I didn't want to look at but looked at anyway. Pedro Infante was about to burst into song, and my father was laughing. I'm not sure if it was because my story was translated into Spanish, or because it was published in Mexico, or perhaps because the story dealt with **Tepeyac**⑫, the *colonia* my father was raised in and the house he grew up in, but at any rate, my father punched the mute button on his remote control and read my story.

18   I sat on the bed next to my father and waited. He read it very slowly. As if he were reading each line over and over. He laughed at all the right places and read lines he liked out loud. He pointed and asked questions: "Is this So-and-so?" "Yes," I said. He kept reading.

19   When he was finally finished, after what seemed like hours, my father looked up and asked: "Where can we get more copies of this for the relatives?"

20   Of all the wonderful things that happened to me last year, that was the most wonderful.

Notes

① **Es maestro**   She is a teacher.
② **profesora**   professor
③ **Alarma**   Alarm
④ **La Virgen de Guadalupe**   The Virgin of Guadalupe, Mexican icon and object of religious veneration, 墨西哥一座圣山,因一圣女在那里显灵而闻名
⑤ **fotonovelas**   photo-novels
⑥ **National Endowment for the Arts Fellowship**   money grant from a prominent organization that supports the arts, 国家艺术奖学金
⑦ **the University of California, at Berkeley**   first and most well-known campus of the University of California system, 美国加州大学伯克利分校
⑧ **tamales**   Mexican dish of shredded meat and peppers wrapped in corn husks, 蕉叶玉米粽子 (此处为复数形式)
⑨ **Pedro Infante** (1917—1957)   Mexican singer and actor, (人名) 墨西哥20世纪40年代著名的男歌星和影星
⑩ **Galavision**   Hispanic television network, 拉美一家电视台
⑪ **Kleenex**   brand name of facial tissue, 克力内克斯面巾纸(商标名)

⑫ **Tepeyac** region near Mexico City where the Virgin of Guadalupe was sighted, 墨西哥一地名, Guadalupe 山就坐落在那里

Exercises

A. Answer the following questions on the text.

1. According to the selection, exactly what did it mean to be "only a daughter" in a Mexican or working-class family? What were Cisneros's family's expectations for her?
2. Cisneros writes that when she heard her father say, "I have seven sons," she "could feel [herself] being erased." What does she mean by "being erased"? What might parents of all cultures learn from this comment?
3. Cisneros' father doesn't read the sort of material she writes. In fact, he doesn't even read English. Yet his daughter states, "In a sense, everything I have ever written has been for him." What does she mean, and why do you think she feels this way?

B. Choose the best answer to each of the following questions.

1. The word "destiny" in "Being only a daughter for my father meant my destiny would lead me to become someone's wife" (Paragraph 4) means _____.
   A. health   B. fate   C. beauty   D. intelligence
2. The word "philandering" in "a wife's revenge on her philandering husband by bashing his skull in" (Paragraph 7) means _____.
   A. hardworking   B. unattractive   C. loving   D. unfaithful
3. Which of the following would be a good alternative title for this selection?
   A. Why I Went to College
   B. My First Published Story
   C. Fathers and Daughters
   D. How I Eventually Gained My Father's Approval
4. Which of the following sentences best expresses the main idea of the selection?
   A. Cisneros' father believed daughters were meant for husbands.
   B. Cisneros always wanted to be a writer.
   C. Cisneros wanted her father to recognize her ability, and she finally succeeded.
   D. Despite her successes, Cisneros has remained true to her family and her Mexican heritage.
5. As a child, Cisneros _____.
   A. enjoyed playing outside with her six brothers
   B. spent a great deal of time alone
   C. had to go to work to help support her family
   D. did not want to go to college
6. Cisneros and her family moved often because _____.
   A. they wanted to live in a neighborhood with good schools
   B. they disliked living in Chicago

C. her father missed his homeland

D. they were unable to pay the rent

7. The author says that to her father majoring in English was _____.

A. acceptable for a daughter, but not for a son

B. a waste of education

C. an important achievement

D. a foolish thing for her to do

8. We can assume from Paragraphs 19–21 that Cisneros' father _____.

A. did not understand his daughter's story

B. understood his daughter's story only after she explained it to him

C. was impressed by this particular story because it was related to his life and culture

D. did not like the story but wanted to make his daughter feel good about her work

On-the-job Writing: Business Letters

Most traditional business letters are neatly typed on one side of 8 1/2-by-11-inch white bond paper（证券纸，高级书写用纸）. Margins are usually set for a minimum of 11/4 inches at the top and at least once inch on the left and right sides and at the bottom. Almost all professional letters now use the "block form"—that is, lines of type are flush with the left margin（左对齐） and paragraphs are not indented（缩格）. Envelopes should match the letter paper.

Business letters typically have six primary parts: heading, inside address, salutation, text, complementary close, signature.

1. The **heading** of a letter is your address and the date, typed either above the inside address of the letter or in the upper right corner. If the heading is in the upper right position, the longest line should end at the one-inch margin on the right side of the page. All lines in your heading should begin evenly on the left. If you are using letterhead stationary (paper already imprinted with your business name, address, or logo), you need to add only the date.

2. The **inside address** contains the name of the person to whom you are writing, the person's title or position, the name of the company or organization, the full address (street or post office box, city, state, ZIP Code). The first line of the inside address should appear at least two spaces below the last line of the heading. (The inside address information should be repeated exactly on your letter's envelope.) If a person's title has more than two words, put it on a separate line.

3. The **salutation** is your letter's greeting to your reader. Begin the salutation two spaces down from the inside address, and greet the person formally using the word "Dear" plus title and name (Dear Mr. Smith, Dear Ms. Jones, Dear Dr. Black). The salutation is traditionally followed by a colon rather than the more informal comma.

4. The **text** of your letter refers to the message that appears in the paragraphs. As in essays, think of your text as having a beginning, a middle, and an ending.

Because professional people receive so much mail, business letters should be brief and to the point.

If possible, keep your letter to one page. If you must go to a second page, type your name, the date, and the page number in an upper corner. Second and subsequent pages should be plain paper, without letterhead material.

5. The **complimentary closing** of a business letter is a conventional farewell to the reader, typed two spaces below the last line of the text. The two most common phrases for closing formal business correspondence are "Sincerely" and "Yours truly." The fist letter of the first closing word is capitalized（大写）, and the closing is followed by a comma.

6. The **signature part** of a business letter contains both your handwritten name and, beneath that, your typed name. Leave approximately four spaces for your handwritten name, which should be written in black ink.

7. Some letters contain additional information below the signature. Typical notes include the word "enclosure" (or "encl.") to indicate inclusion of additional material (which may be named) or a distribution list to indicate other persons who are receiving a copy of this letter. Distribution is indicated by the word "copy" or by the letter c, cc (for "carbon copy"), or xe (for "Xeroxed copy"), followed by a colon and the name(s); if more than one person is listed, the names should appear in alphabetical order.

Copy:	Mayor Sue Jones	Enclosure *or* Encl.
	or	*or*
cc:	Mayor Sue Jones,	Enclosure: résumé
	Dr. Inga York	

In formal business correspondence, avoid any sort of postscript (P.S.).

Sample Business Letter

Art Tech Studio
802 West Street
Fort Collins, CO 80525
May 10, 2018

Mr. Thomas Valdez
General Manager
Harmony Product, Inc.
645 Monroe Avenue
Little Rock, AR 90056

Dear Mr. Valdez:

Thank you for your May 5 order for twenty of my hand-designed laptop cases and for your advance payment check of $250. I am delighted that your company wishes to stock my painted carrying case in both your Little Rock and Fayetteville stores.

The cases are being packed in individual boxes this week and should arrive by Air Flight Mail at your main office no later than May 25. If you wish for me to use express-mail for quicker delivery, please let me know.

Many thanks again for your interest in my work and for your recent order. I am planning to attend a marketing seminar in Little Rock, June 5–8; I will call you next week to see if we might arrange a brief meeting at your convenience on one of those days. Until then, should you need to contact me, please call my studio (970/555-6009).

Sincerely,

Rachel Zimmerman

Rachel Zimmerman

Enclosure: receipt

Unit Three

Text A

Pre-reading Activities

1. Are you aware that the world is full of advertisements? Are you aware that advertisements are shaping our opinions and decisions?
2. Advertisements work because they use many techniques in getting across their messages. What techniques have you observed?
3. Look at an advertisement in a magazine or on television and try to discover how it makes you believe what it wants you to believe.

Propaganda Techniques in Advertising
Ann McClintock

1 We Americans, adults and children alike, are being seduced. We are being brainwashed. And few of us protest. Why? Because the seducers and the brainwashers are the advertisers we willingly invite into our homes. We are victims, seemingly content—even eager—to be victimized. One study reports that each of us, during an average day, is exposed to over *five hundred* advertising claims of various types. This bombardment may even increase in the future, since current trends include ads on movie screens, shopping carts, videocassettes, even public television. We read advertisers' messages in newspapers and magazines; we watch their alluring images on television. We absorb their messages into our subconscious.

2 Advertisers lean heavily on propaganda to sell their products, whether the "product" is a brand of toothpaste, a candidate for office, or a political viewpoint. *Propaganda* is a systematic effort to influence people's opinions, to win them over to a certain view or side. Propaganda is not necessarily concerned with what is true or false, good or bad. Propagandists simply want people to believe the messages being sent. Advertisers often use subtle deceptions to sway people's opinions; they may even use what amount to outright lies.

3 What kind of propaganda techniques do advertisers use? There are seven common types:

4 **Name-Calling**. Name-calling is a propaganda tactic in which a competitor is referred to with negatively charged names or comments. By using such negative associations, propagandists try to arouse feelings of mistrust, fear, and even hate in their audiences. For example, a political advertisement may label an opposing candidate a "loser," "fence-sitter,"

or "warmonger." Depending on the advertiser's target market, labels such as "a friend of big business" or "a dues-paying member of the party in power" can be the epithets that damage an opponent. Ads for products also often use name-calling. An American manufacturer may refer in its commercial, for instance, to a "foreign car"— not an "imported one." The label of foreignness will have unpleasant connotations in many people's minds. Another example is the **MasterCard**① ad that shows a man trying unsuccessfully to get some cash with his **American Express**② card. A childhood rhyme claims that "names can never hurt me," but name-calling is an effective way to damage the opposition, whether it is another credit card company or a congressional candidate.

5　　**Glittering Generalities**. A glittering generality is an important-sounding but general claim for which no explanation or proof is offered. It is the opposite of name-calling. Advertisers who use glittering generalities surround their products with attractive — and slippery — words and phrases. They use vague terms that are difficult to define and that may have different meanings to different people, such as "great," "progress," "beautiful," and "super." This kind of language stirs positive feelings in people, feelings that may spill over to the product or idea being pitched. As with name-calling, the emotional response may overwhelm logic. Target audiences accept the product without thinking very much about what the glittering generalities really mean.

6　　The ads for politicians and political causes often use glittering generalities because such buzzwords can influence votes. Election slogans include high-sounding but basically empty phrases like the following:

7　　"He cares about people." (That's nice, but is he a better candidate than his opponent?)
　　"Vote for progress." (Progress by *whose* standards?)
　　"They'll make this country great again." (Does "great" mean the same thing to the candidate as it does to me?)
　　"Vote for the future." (What kind of future?)

8　　Ads for consumer goods are also sprinkled with generalities. Product names, for instance, are often designed to evoke good feelings: *Loves* diapers, *New Freedom* feminine hygiene products, *Joy* liquid detergent, and *Loving Care* hair color. Product slogans lean heavily on vague but comforting phrases: **Kinney**③ is "The Great American Shoe Store," **General Electric**④ "brings good things to life," and **Dow Chemical**⑤ "lets you do great things." We are also told that **Chevrolet**⑥ is the "heartbeat of America" and Coke is "the real thing."

9　　**Transfer**. In transfer, advertisers try to improve the image of a product by associating it with a symbol or image most people respect and admire, like the American flag or Uncle Sam. The advertisers hope that the trust and prestige attached to the symbol or image will carry over to the product. Many companies use transfer devices to identify their products: Lincoln Insurance shows a profile of the president; Continental Insurance portrays a **Revolutionary War Minuteman**⑦; **Amtrak**⑧'s logo is red, white, and blue; **Liberty Mutual**⑨'s corporate symbol is the **Statue of Liberty**⑩; **Allstate**⑪'s name is cradled by a pair of protective, fatherly hands.

10   Corporations also use the transfer technique when they sponsor prestigious shows on radio and television. These shows function as symbols of dignity and class. **Kraft Corporation**[12], for instance, sponsored a **Leonard Bernstein**[13] *Conducts Beethoven*[14] concert, while Gulf Oil is the sponsor of **National Geographic**[15] specials and **Mobil**[16] supports public television's *Masterpiece Theater*. In this way, corporations reach an educated, influential audience and improve their public image by associating themselves with quality programming.

11   Political candidates, of course, practically wrap themselves in the flag. Ads for a candidate often show either the **Washington Monument**[17], a **Fourth of July**[18] parade, the **Stars and Stripes**[19], or a bald eagle soaring over the mountains. The national anthem or "America the Beautiful" may play softly in the background. Such appeals to Americans' love of country surround the candidate with an aura of patriotism and integrity.

12   **Testimonial**. The testimonial is one of advertisers' most-used propaganda techniques. Similar to the transfer device, the testimonial capitalizes on the admiration people have for a celebrity—even though the celebrity is not an expert on the product being sold.

13   Print and television ads offer a nonstop parade of testimonials: here's **Cher**[20] for **Holiday Spas**[21]; here's basketball star **Michael Jordan**[22] eating **Wheaties**[23]; **Michael Jackson**[24] sings about Pepsi; American Express features a slew of well-known people who assure us that they never go anywhere without their American Express card. Testimonials can sell movies, too; newspaper ads for films often feature favorable comments by well-known reviewers. And, in recent years, testimonials have played an important role in pitching books; the backs of paperbacks frequently list complimentary blurbs by celebrities.

14   As illogical as testimonials sometimes are (Pepsi's Michael Jackson, for instance, is a health-food adherent who does not drink soft drinks), they are effective propaganda. We like the *person* so much we like the *product* too.

15   **Plain Folks**. The plain folks approach says, in effect, "Buy me or vote for me. I'm just like you." Regular folks will surely like **Bob Evans**[25]'s Down on the Farm Country Sausage or good old-fashioned Country Time Lemonade. Some ads emphasize the idea that "we're all in the same boat." We see people making long-distance calls for just the reasons we do—to put the baby on the phone to Grandma or to tell Mom we love her. And how do these folksy, warmhearted scenes affect us? They're supposed to make us feel that **AT&T**[26]—the multinational corporate giant—has the same values we do. Similarly, we are introduced to the "little people" at Ford, the ordinary folks who work on the assembly line, not to bigwigs in their executive offices. What's the purpose of such an approach? To encourage us to buy a car built by these honest, hardworking "everyday Joes" who care about quality as much as we do.

16   Political advertisements make almost as much use of the "plain folks" appeal as they do of transfer devices. Candidates wear hard hats, farmers' caps, and assembly-line

coveralls. They jog around the block and carry their own luggage through the airport. The idea is to convince voters that the candidates are at heart average people with the same values, goals, and needs as you and I have.

17　　**Card Stacking.** When people say that "the cards were stacked against me," they mean that they were never given a fair chance. Applied to propaganda, card stacking means telling half-truths—misrepresenting the facts by suppressing relevant evidence. Card stacking is a difficult form of propaganda both to detect and to combat. When a candidate claims that an opponent has "changed his mind three times on this important issue," we tend to accept the claim without investigating whether the candidate had good reasons for changing his mind. Many people are simply swayed by the implication that the candidate is "waffling" on the issue.

18　　Advertisers also use a card-stacking trick when they make an unfinished claim. For example, they will say that their product has "twice as much pain reliever." We are left with a favorable impression. We don't usually ask, "Twice as much pain reliever as what?" When **Ford**[20] claimed that its LTD model was "400 percent quieter," many people assumed that the LTD must be quieter than all other cars. When taken to court, however, Ford admitted that the phrase referred to the difference between the noise level inside and outside the LTD.

19　　**Bandwagon.** In the bandwagon technique, advertisers urge, "Everyone's doing it. Why don't you?" This kind of propaganda appeals to the deep desire many have not to be different. Political ads tell us to vote for the "winning candidate." Advertisers know we tend to feel comfortable doing what others do; we want to be on the winning team. Or ads show a series of people proclaiming, "I'm voting for the Senator. I don't know why anyone wouldn't." Again, the audience feels under pressure to conform.

20　　The bandwagon approach is also a staple of consumer ads. They tell us, for example, that "Nobody doesn't like Sara Lee" (the message is that you must be weird if you don't). They tell us that "Most people prefer Brand X two to one over other leading brands" (to be like the majority, we should buy Brand X). If we don't drink Pepsi, we're left out of "the Pepsi generation." To take part in "America's favorite health kick," the National Dairy Council urges us to drink milk. And Honda motorcycle ads, praising the virtues of being a follower, tell us, "Follow the leader. He's on a Honda."

21　　Why do these propaganda techniques work? Why do so many of us buy the products, viewpoints, and candidates urged on us by propaganda messages? They work because they appeal to our emotions, not to our minds. Clear thinking requires hard work: analyzing a claim, researching the facts, examining both sides of an issue, using logic to see the flaws in an argument. Many of us would rather let the propagandists do our thinking for us. Because propaganda is so effective, it is important to detect it and understand how it is used. We may conclude, after close examination, that some propaganda sends a truthful, worthwhile message. Some advertising, for instance, urges us not to drive drunk, to become volunteers, to contribute to charity. We may even agree that a particular soap or soda is "super." Even so, we must be aware that propaganda is being used. Otherwise, we will have consented to handing over to others our independence of thought and action.

Notes

① **MasterCard** credit card, 万事达信用卡
② **American Express** credit card, 美国运通信用卡
③ **Kinney** chain of shoe stores, 曾是美国最大的鞋业零售商
④ **General Electric** large corporation, major supplier of electric appliances, 美国通用电气公司
⑤ **Dow Chemical** major research/manufacturer of chemicals and plastics, 陶氏化学公司
⑥ **Chevrolet** one of the "Big Three" auto manufacturers, 美国通用汽车公司生产的雪佛兰汽车
⑦ **Revolutionary War Minuteman** an armed civilian pledged to be ready to fight on a minute's notice, just before and during the Revolutionary War that gained independence from England for the American colonies, 战争期间召之即来的民兵
⑧ **Amtrak** United States railroad system, 美国一家铁路运输公司
⑨ **Liberty Mutual** insurance company, 美国利宝互助保险公司
⑩ **Statue of Liberty** United States National Monument in New York Harbor, symbolizing freedom and democracy, 自由女神像
⑪ **Allstate** insurance company, 美国一家保险公司
⑫ **Kraft Corporation** major manufacturer of processed foods, 卡夫食品公司
⑬ **Leonard Bernstein** (1918—1990) long-time music director and conductor of the New York Philharmonic Orchestra and composer, 伯恩斯坦, 美国指挥家、作曲家
⑭ **Ludwig van Beethoven** (1770—1827) German composer and pianist, 贝多芬（1770 - 1827）, 德国作曲家
⑮ ***National Geographic*** magazine produced by the National Geographic Society, which is known for its promotion of geography, world cultures, botany, zoology, and for its magazine of excellent photographic essays, 美国《国家地理》杂志
⑯ **Mobil** major oil company, 美孚石油公司
⑰ **Washington Monument** United States National Monument in Washington, D.C., commemorating the first president of the United States, George Washington, 华盛顿纪念碑
⑱ **Fourth of July** United States national holiday celebrating independence, 7月4日, 美国独立日
⑲ **the Stars and Stripes** the United States flag, 星条旗, 美国国旗
⑳ **Cher** (1946—) 原名 Cherilyn Sarkisian LaPiere, American pop star and all-around entertainer, 美国著名演员、歌手
㉑ **Holiday Spas** chain of health spas offering fitness and beauty services at premier resort venues, 假期水疗美容

㉒ **Michael Jordan** (1963—)　much celebrated NBA basketball star, most often associated with the Chicago Bulls, the team he led to numerous titles, 迈克尔·乔丹，美国著名篮球运动员

㉓ **Wheaties**　breakfast cereal touted as "Breakfast of Champions," 一种早餐用的谷物食物著名品牌

㉔ **Michael Jackson** (1958—2009)　dominant figure in pop culture, also of popular interest because of facial alterations and 2007 lawsuits, 迈克尔·杰克逊，美国著名通俗歌手

㉕ **Bob Evans** (1918—)　Restaurant founder Bob Evans was born on May 30, 1918, in Sugar Ridge, Ohio. Evans ventured into the restaurant business in the 1940s, operating a small diner. What made a name for his restaurant was his sausage, produced from his own hogs. Eventually, the Bob Evans name became synonymous with both sausage and country-style restaurants. 美国一家连锁饭店创始人，该店以自制香肠闻名。

㉖ **AT & T**　major player in the communications industry, 美国电报电话公司

㉗ **Ford**　one of the original producers of automobiles and still one of the "Big Three", 福特汽车公司

Vocabulary

1. seduce　[sɪˈdjuːs]　*vt.* to tempt or persuade someone to do something against his or her will or better judgment, 引诱
2. brainwash　[ˈbreɪnwɒʃ]　*vt.* to subject to indoctrination, 洗脑
3. victim　[ˈvɪktɪm]　*n.* a person tricked or fooled or harmed, 受害者，上当受骗者
4. victimize　[ˈvɪktɪmaɪz]　*vt.* to trick or harm someone, 使……受害、受苦
5. bombardment　[bɒmˈbɑːdm(ə)nt]　*n.* an attack with missiles, guns; a persistent barrage of words or requests, 攻击
6. alluring　[əˈl(j)ʊərɪŋ]　*adj.* attractive, charming, 诱惑的，迷惑的
7. absorb　[əbˈzɔːb; -ˈsɔːb]　*vt.* to take in and assimilate, 吸收
8. subconscious　[sʌbˈkɒnʃəs]　*n. & adj.* concerning the thoughts or instincts in the mind of which the person is not fully aware, 潜意识，下意识
9. lean　[liːn]　*vi.* stand slanting, to bend or incline, 倾斜，弯曲
10. propaganda　[prɒpəˈɡændə]　*n.* systematic efforts to spread ideas, opinions, and thoughts by appealing to the emotions, 宣传，传播
11. systematic　[sɪstəˈmætɪk]　*adj.* according to a system, methodical, 系统的，有秩序的
12. sway　[sweɪ]　*vt.* to move from side to side; to have influence or change opinions, 影响，改变（观点）
13. outright　[ˈaʊtraɪt]　*adj.* without any doubt, unmistakably, openly, completely, 毫无疑义的，断然的，清楚的
14. tactic　[ˈtæktɪk]　*n.* means of achieving a desired result, method, 策略，手段，方法
15. charged　[tʃɑːdʒd]　*adj.* filled with, loaded with, 充满的，装满的

16. label ['leɪb(ə)l] *vt.* to identify as to owner or content, 贴标签,标记
17. fence-sitter ['fenssɪtə] *n.* one who takes a position of neutrality or indecision, as in a controversial matter, 摇摆不定,骑墙派
18. warmonger ['wɔːmʌŋɡə] *n.* someone, especially a politician, who promotes war, used to show disapproval, 战争贩子〈贬义〉
19. epithet ['epɪθet] *n.* a phrase expressing an attribute or quality of something, （描述特征的）短语
20. connotation [kɒnəˈteɪʃ(ə)n] *n.* the implied or suggested meaning in addition to the simple or literal meaning, overtone, 外延,言外之意,隐含之意
21. congressional [kənˈɡreʃənəl] *adj.* referring to the United States Congress, （有关）国会的
22. glitter ['ɡlɪtə] *vi.* to shine, sparkle, 闪烁,闪耀,闪光
23. generality [dʒenəˈrælɪtɪ] *n.* vague, indefinite and general statement, 概述,泛泛之说
24. slippery ['slɪp(ə)rɪ] *adj.* difficult to grasp, as in having a smooth surface; elusive and hard to catch, 光滑的;不可靠的
25. pitch [pɪtʃ] *vt.* to promote or sell, （以某种方式）表达（某事物）
26. overwhelm [əʊvəˈwelm] *vt.* overcome completely, crush, 压倒,制服
27. sprinkle ['sprɪŋk(ə)l] *vi.* to randomly spray or cover with small drops or particles, 撒,洒,散布（东西）
28. evoke [ɪˈvəʊk] *vi.* to call forth, bring out, 唤起,引起（感情或回忆）
29. buzzword ['bʌzwɜːd] *n.* a catchword, a popular word or a phrase, sometimes within a particular business, 流行语,流行术语
30. hygiene ['haɪdʒiːn] *n.* the science or practice of keeping healthy and clean, 卫生（学）
31. heartbeat ['hɑːtbiːt] *n.* pulsation of the heart; the main source of the activities, 心跳;（活动）主要来源
32. transfer [trænsˈfɜː; trɑːns-; -nz-] *vi.* to move something from one place to another, 转移
33. cradle ['kreɪd(ə)l] *vt.* to hold protectively, 将……（如同）置于摇篮中
34. insurance [ɪnˈʃʊər(ə)ns] *n.* the business of covering losses of property, person, or life, 保险（业）
35. profile ['prəʊfaɪl] *n.* side view of the face, outline, 侧面（像）,轮廓;人物简介
36. sponsor ['spɒnsə] *vt.* to assume responsibility for, to support, 赞助或担保,倡仪
37. prestigious [preˈstɪdʒəs] *adj.* having an excellent reputation, worthy of respect, 享有声誉的,有名望的,有影响力的
38. wrap [ræp] *vt.* to cover by folding or winding around, 包,裹（东西）
39. aura ['ɔːrə] *n.* an invisible but noticeable quality surrounding a person or thing, 光环,光晕
40. patriotism ['peɪtrɪətɪz(ə)m] *n.* love of one's country and readiness to defend it, 爱国主义
41. integrity [ɪnˈteɡrɪtɪ] *n.* the quality of being honest, moral uprightness; whole, undivided, 正直,诚实（的品格）;完整,整体
42. testimonial [ˌtestɪˈməʊnɪəl] *n.* a statement or act to show admiration, worthiness, or respect; a tribute, 推荐或赞扬的行为;证明书,推荐书

43. capitalize [ˈkæpɪtəlaɪz] *vi.* turn into capital, e.g., money, shares, investment, 变成资本,用作资本
44. celebrity [sɪˈlebrɪtɪ] *n.* a famous person, especially in pop culture, 名人
45. feature [ˈfiːtʃə] *vt.* to give prominence to, to give special attention to, 突出；主演
46. complimentary [kɒmplɪˈment(ə)rɪ] *adj.* expressing admiration, praise, or respect for,（表示）赞誉的,称赞的,赞许的
47. blurb [blɜːb] *n.* a brief advertisement or description full of high praise, especially on the jacket of a book, album, or other packaged items for sale, 充满溢美之词的小广告或描述（常出现在出售的书、相册的背面或其他物件的外包装上）
48. folk [fəʊk] *n.* people in general, common people, 人,人们,平常人
49. approach [əˈprəʊtʃ] *n.* method of working on a problem,（解决问题的）方法,方案
50. assembly [əˈsemblɪ] *n.* a coming together of a group of people; process of fitting together the parts of something, 集会；装配,组装
51. bigwig [ˈbɪgwɪg] *n. informal* an important person, 〈非正式用法〉重要人物
52. executive [ɪgˈzekjʊtɪv] *n.* person or group in a business organization with administrative power, manager,（企业等）行政领导,经理
53. coveralls [ˈkʌvəˈɔːlz] *n.* loose-fitting protective garment, 工作裤
54. stack [stæk] *vt.* to pile or arrange or build in a stack, 堆,垒
55. detect [dɪˈtekt] *v.* to find out something hidden; discover, 察觉,发现,侦查
56. combat [ˈkɒmbæt; ˈkʌm-] *v.* to fight against, to struggle against, 战斗,斗争
57. waffling [ˈwɒflɪŋ] *adj.* vague, indecisive, changing one's mind on an issue, 〈非正式用法〉模糊的,不确切的
58. reliever [rɪˈliːvə] *n.* a person or thing that lessens pain or distress,（解除痛苦或危险等的）人或事物
59. bandwagon [ˈbændwægən] *n.* popular trend which everyone is expected to accept, 〈非正式,引申用法〉流行行为,通行做法
60. conform [kənˈfɔːm] *vi & vt.* to act according to law or rule, in agreement with generally accepted standards, 遵循,依循,保持一致
61. staple [ˈsteɪp(ə)l] *n.* basic or principal item or element, 主要内容,主要成分
62. consumer [kənˈsjuːmə] *n.* a person who buys the products made by producers, 消费者
63. charity [ˈtʃærɪtɪ] *n.* generous giving to the needy or to organizations looking after the poor or sick, 慈善行为
64. consent [kənˈsent] *vi.* to agree, to give approval or permission, 同意,允许

Useful Expressions

1. **expose ... to:** to make liable to, be open to

   (1) The report showed that the workers had been exposed to a dangerous environment.

   (2) The children were exposed to fever because one of their classmates was ill.

2. **lean on:** to depend on, rely on
   (1) The family leaned on each other for support in this hard time.
   (2) Some businessmen lean heavily on their social connections to promote their businesses.
3. **win over:** to get support or friendship
   (1) The candidate asked everybody in the team to work hard to win over those undecided votes.
   (2) His excellent performance in this film helped to win over some audiences.
4. **amount to:** to be equal to, have the same effect
   (1) The measure the government took in the economic crisis amounted to nothing.
   (2) If you do it in this way, it will only amount to doing it over again, which is useless.
5. **attach ... to:** to be part of, to work for a part of an organization
   (1) I used to work for the high school attached to the university.
   (2) He was attached to a department in an American newspaper.
6. **associate ... with:** to make a mental connection with
   (1) In North America, some people associate turkey with Thanksgiving.
   (2) I don't think I can associate him with academic research.
7. **carry over:** If something is carried over into a new situation, it continues to exist in the new situation.
   (1) The pain and violence of his childhood were carried over into his marriage.
   (2) I try not to let my problems at work carry over into my private life.
8. **a slew of:** (*informal*) a large number of
   (1) On the two sides of the highway is a slew of cheap hotels.
   (2) A slew of celebrities is present at today's press conference.
9. **in effect:** in essence, in fact, for all purposes
   (1) In effect, we will meet with more difficulties in our work this year than last year.
   (2) The two approaches to this problem are in effect the same.
10. **at heart:** in nature, in fact
    (1) She is already in her late sixties, but is young and romantic at heart.
    (2) At heart Tom may be a working class boy, but in fact he has become an executive.
11. **appeal to:** to have an attraction for; to earnestly ask for help
    (1) Entertainment such as movies and popular songs always appeals to one's emotions rather than to one's reason.
    (2) When I told my son "No," he would appeal to his mother.
12. **capitalize on:** to take advantage of, make use of
    (1) One suggestion is that the county should capitalize on its natural beauty to attract tourists.
    (2) Why don't we capitalize on people's expectations for the "new" and the "free" to promote our product?
13. **be left out (of)/ leave out:** to be excluded/to exclude
    (1) Jim has been left out of the team because he has not attended its practice many times.
    (2) She has been very careful in organizing the party, hoping not to leave anything out.

14. **hand over / hand... over (to):** to transfer authority, to give over

   (1) The soldiers were ordered to hand over their guns after they lost the battle.

   (2) After my retirement, I will hand my business over to my son.

15. **consent to:** to give permission for something

   (1) The father reluctantly consented to the daughter's marriage.

   (2) Democratic audiences had to consent to this approach.

Understaning the Text

1. Why does the author say that Americans are being brainwashed?
2. What is propaganda according to the text?
3. Some of the propaganda techniques listed in the selection have contrasting appeal. How do the "name-calling" and "glittering generalities" approaches contrast each other? How do the "testimonial" and "plain folks" strategies contrast each other?
4. As a propaganda technique, how does "transfer" work?
5. What is card-stacking in propaganda?
6. Why are ads with a bandwagon appeal so effective? What ads have you seen lately that use this technique?

Exercises

A. Fill in the blanks with the appropriate words from the text.

1. We Americans are being seduced and brainwashed and few of us protest because the seducers and the brainwashers are the advertisers we _____ invite into our homes. We _____ messages in newspapers and magazines, we _____ their alluring images on television. We _____ their messages into our subconscious.

2. People use vague terms that are difficult to define and may have different meanings to different people such as _____, _____, _____ and _____. This kind of language _____ positive feelings in people, feelings that may _____ to the product or idea being pitched. The emotional response may _____ logic. Target audiences accept the product _____ thinking very much about what the glittering generalities really mean.

3. We are introduced to the "little people" at Ford, ordinary _____ who work on the assembly line, not bigwigs in their executive offices. The purpose is to encourage us to buy a car built by these honest, hardworking _____ who care about quality as much as we do.

4. The propaganda of advertisements works because they appeal to our _____, not to our _____. Clear thinking requires hard work: _____ a claim, _____

the facts, _____ both sides of an issue, _____ logic to see the flaws in an argument.

B. Choose from the words given below to complete the following sentences, changing the word form where necessary.

alike	label	vague	appeal
sway	prestigious	evoke	arouse
charged	urge	conform	feature

1. Dolly writes with eloquence about the _____ of the Jewish faith for her.
2. Politicians and voters _____ are too concerned with short-term problems.
3. His strange behavior _____ the suspicions of the police.
4. A new blockbuster has been just released _____ a couple of well-known Hollywood actors and actresses.
5. The congressional candidate gave many promises which may _____ people's decision in voting.
6. I've only got a _____ idea of what he wants for this project.
7. A good joke usually _____ much laughter.
8. If you wish to be a member, you must _____ to the rules of our club.
9. She is a partner in one of New York's oldest and most _____ law firms.
10. Please _____ the place settings with the names of the guests and put them on the table in order.
11. Abortion is still a very emotionally _____ issue in the U.S.
12. She _____ upon him the need for extreme secrecy.

C. Fill in the blanks with the phrases given below, changing the form where necessary.

expose... to	in effect	a slew of	refer to
associate with	attach... to	win over	carry over
lean on	hand over	care about	consent to
at heart	leave out	appeal to	

1. She did a good presentation at today's meeting except that one minor detail _____.
2. The British government _____ Hong Kong to the Chinese government in 1997, which was a great event for the Chinese people.
3. _____ well-known people attended today's opening ceremony.
4. His excessive weight _____ him _____ a lot of joking at the office.
5. In the past, people would _____ jiaozi _____ the Spring Festival in China.
6. The program showed that the officials were _____ ordinary people like everybody else, but in fact they were not.
7. To get support is one thing, to _____ people's hearts is another thing.
8. The recovery of the stock market _____ the confidence of the investors, I suppose.

9. The world leaders ought to re-consider the policy of _____ arms to settle the disputes between countries.
10. _____, the criminals have already been punished without trials.
11. And obviously, if we feel this way about something as small as ordering at a restaurant, it can influence and _____ to the big things in our lives.
12. After fierce discussion, the whole class finally _____ the proposal raised by the little girl to come to school an hour later than usual time.

D. Fill in the blanks with the expressions given below, changing the form where necessary.

alluring images	public image	fair chance
an average day	ordinary folks	deep desire
important sounding	assembly line	clear thinking
target audiences	average people	

1. One report said that on _____ it took two hours to get around town, indicating the worsening of traffic jams.
2. Behind the consumption activities lies the _____ of consumers to "catch up with the Jones."
3. During travel I prefer meeting _____ to visiting sites of interest and scenic spots.
4. With the coming of the Olympic Games, the city has taken many measures to improve its _____.
5. Not only hard work but also _____ is required to detect the false messages in many ads.
6. In fact it is the _____ not the celebrities who are supporting the entertainment industry.
7. The _____ is the symbol of industrialization while the computer is the hallmark of the information age.
8. All soap operas have their _____; that's why they are always welcome to some viewers.
9. I found out the product was not the same as its _____ on TV.
10. The project is _____ but lacks the support to be carried out.

E. Read the following text and choose the best word for each blank from the choices given.

Advertisers' use of doublespeak is endless. Rosser Reeves has explained advertising's function this way: to make (1) _____ out of nothing. The best way advertisers can make something out of nothing is (2) _____ words. Although there are a lot of visual images used on television and in magazines and (3) _____, every advertiser wants to create that memorable line that will stick in the public's (4) _____.

The variations, combinations, and permutations of doublespeak used in advertising go on and on, running from the use of rhetorical questions ("Wouldn't you really rather have a Buick?") (5) _____ flattering you with compliments ("The lady has taste. We think a cigar smoker is someone special."). You know, of course, how you're (6) _____ to answer those questions, and you know that those compliments are just leading up to the sales pitches for the products. (7) _____ you dismiss such tricks of the trade as obvious, however, just remember that all of these statements and questions were part of very successful advertising campaigns.

A more subtle approach is the ad that proclaims a supposedly unique quality for a product, a quality that (8) _____ isn't unique. "If it doesn't say Goodyear, it can't be Polyglas." Sounds good, doesn't it? Polyglas is available only from Goodyear because Goodyear copyrighted that trade name. Any other tire manufacturer could make exactly the (9) _____ tire but could not call it Polyglas, because that (10) _____ be copyright infringement. Polyglas is simply Goodyear's name for its fiberglass-reinforced tire.

1. A. something   B. good   C. profit   D. money
2. A. for   B. with   C. through   D. of
3. A. newspapers   B. articles   C. essays   D. journals
4. A. mind   B. awareness   C. consciousness   D. heart
5. A. the   B. to   C. do   D. leading
6. A. supposed   B. asked   C. forced   D. demanded
7. A. After   B. Before   C. Since   D. As
8. A. very   B. really   C. much   D. extremely
9. A. different   B. proper   C. same   D. similar
10. A. would   B. will   C. may   D. might

F. Translate the following sentences into English, using the phrases and expressions given in parentheses.

1. 有些广告的成功在于充分利用了人们崇拜名人的心理。(capitalize on)
2. 要把这么大的一个企业交给一个二十几岁的年轻人我还真有点不放心。(hand over)
3. 这个节目的目的是要告诉观众这些英雄们在本质上和我们一样,都是平常人。(at heart)
4. 诉诸理智而不是情感,这是处理矛盾的一个基本原则。(appeal to)
5. 和一种情形关联的情感很容易转移到别的情形中。(attach to)
6. 长时间在阳光下暴露皮肤容易得皮肤癌,这也是我不喜欢在海滩上晒太阳的原因。(expose to)
7. 越是在艰难环境里,越要互相依赖,才能最后克服困难。(lean on)
8. 在这次选举中,我们的策略是先赢得民众的信任,然后获得他们的支持。(win over)
9. 在这个公司里,经理的话就跟命令差不多。(amount to)
10. 报告的内容很多,但是篇幅有限,所以不得不省略不少细节。(leave out)

Text B

With These Words I Can Sell You Anything
William Lutz[①]

1. One problem advertisers have when they try to convince you that the product they are pushing is really different from other similar products is that their claims are subject to some laws. Not a lot of laws, but there are some designed to prevent fraudulent or untruthful claims in advertising. Even during the happy years of non-regulation under President Ronald Reagan, the **FTC**[②] did crack down on the more blatant abuses in advertising claims. Generally speaking, advertisers have to be careful in what they say in the ads, in the claims they make for the products they advertise. Parity claims are safe because they are legal and supported by a number of court decisions. But beyond parity claims there are weasel words.

2. Advertisers use weasel words to appear to be making a claim for a product when in fact they are making no claim at all. Weasel words get their name from the way weasels eat the eggs they find in the nests of other animals. A weasel will make a small hole in the egg, suck out the insides, then place the egg back in the nest. Only when the egg is examined closely is it found to be hollow. That's the way it is with weasel words in advertising: Examine weasel words closely and you'll find that they're as hollow as any egg sucked by a weasel. Weasel words appear to say one thing when in fact they say the opposite, or nothing at all.

Help—*The* Number One Weasel Word

3. The biggest weasel word used in advertising doublespeak is *help*. Now *help* only means to aid or assist, nothing more. It does not mean to conquer, stop, eliminate, end, solve, heal, cure, or anything else. But once the ad says *help*, it can say just about anything after that because *help* qualifies everything coming after it. The trick is that the claim that comes after the weasel word is usually so strong and so dramatic that you forget the word *help* and concentrate only on the dramatic claim. You read into the ad a message that the ad does not contain. More importantly, the advertiser is not responsible for the claim that you read into the ad, even though the advertiser wrote the ad so you would read that claim into it.

4. The next time you see an ad for a cold medicine that promises that it "helps relieve cold symptoms fast," don't rush out to buy it. Ask yourself what this claim is really saying. Remember, *helps* means only that the medicine will aid or assist. What will it aid or assist in doing? Why, "relieve" your cold "symptoms." *Relieve* only means to ease, alleviate, or mitigate, not to stop, end, or cure. Nor does the claim say how much relieving this medicine will do. Nowhere does this ad claim it will cure anything. In fact, the ad doesn't even claim it will do anything at all. The ad only claims that it will aid in relieving (not curing) your cold

symptoms, which are probably a runny nose, watery eyes, and a headache. In other words, this medicine probably contains a standard decongestant and some aspirin. By the way, what does *fast* mean? Ten minutes, one hour, one day? What is fast to one person can be very slow to another. *Fast* is another weasel word.

5 Ad claims using *help* are among the most popular ads. One says, "Helps keep you young looking," but then a lot of things will help keep you young looking, including exercise, rest, good nutrition, and a facelift. More importantly, this ad doesn't say the product will keep you young, only "young looking." Someone may look young to one person and old to another.

6 A toothpaste ad says, "Helps prevent cavities," but it doesn't say it will actually prevent cavities. Brushing your teeth regularly, avoiding sugars in food, and flossing daily will also help prevent cavities. A liquid cleaner ad says, "Helps keep your home germ free," but it doesn't say it actually kills germs, nor does it even specify which germs it might kill.

7 *Help* is such a useful weasel word that it is often combined with other action-verb weasel words such as *fight* and *control*. Consider the claim, "Helps control dandruff symptoms with regular use." What does it really say? It will assist in controlling (not eliminating, stopping, ending, or curing) the *symptoms* of dandruff, not the cause of dandruff nor the dandruff itself. What are the symptoms of dandruff? The ad deliberately leaves that undefined, but assume that the symptoms referred to in the ad are the flaking and itching commonly associated with dandruff. But just shampooing with any shampoo will temporarily eliminate these symptoms, so this shampoo isn't any different from any other. Finally, in order to benefit from this product, you must use it regularly. What is "regular use"—daily, weekly, hourly? Using another shampoo "regularly" will have the same effect. Nowhere does this advertising claim say this particular shampoo stops, eliminates, or cures dandruff. In fact, this claim says nothing at all, thanks to all the weasel words. Look at ads in magazines and newspapers, listen to ads on radio and television, and you'll find the word *help* in ads for all kinds of products. How often do you read or hear such phrases as "helps stop...," "helps overcome...," "helps eliminate...," "helps you feel...," or "helps you look..."? If you start looking for this weasel word in advertising, you'll be amazed at how often it occurs. Analyze the claims in the ads using *help*, and you will discover that these ads are really saying nothing.

8 There are plenty of other weasel words used in advertising. In fact, there are so many that to list them all would fill the rest of this book. But, in order to identify the doublespeak of advertising and understand the real meaning of an ad, you have to be aware of the most popular weasel words in advertising today.

Virtually Spotless

9 One of the most powerful weasel words is *virtually*, a word so innocent that most people don't pay any attention to it when it is used in an advertising claim. But watch out. *Virtually*

is used in advertising claims that appear to make specific, definite promises when there is no promise. After all, what does *virtually* mean? It means "in essence or effect, although not in fact." Look at that definition again. *Virtually* means *not in fact*. It does *not* mean "almost" or "just about the same as," or anything else. And before you dismiss all this concern over such a small word, remember that small words can have big consequences.

10   In 1971, a federal court rendered its decision on a case brought by a woman who became pregnant while taking birth control pills. She sued the manufacturer, Eli Lilly and Company, for breach of warranty. The woman lost her case. Basing its ruling on a statement in the pamphlet accompanying the pills, which stated that "When taken as directed, the tablets offer virtually 100 percent protection," the court ruled that there was no warranty, expressed or implied, that the pills were absolutely effective. In its ruling, the court pointed out that, according to *Webster's Third New International Dictionary*, *virtually* means "almost entirely" and clearly does not mean "absolute." In other words, the Eli Lilly company was really saying that its birth control pill, even when taken as directed, *did not* in fact provide 100 percent protection against pregnancy. But Eli Lilly did not want to put it that way because then many women might not have bought Lilly's birth control pills.

Acts Fast

11   Ads that use such phrases as "acts fast," "acts against," "acts to prevent," and the like are saying essentially nothing, because *act* is a word empty of any specific meaning. The ads are always careful not to specify exactly what "act" the product performs. Just because a brand of aspirin claims to "act fast" for headache relief doesn't mean this aspirin is any better than any other aspirin. What is the "act" that this aspirin performs? You're never told. Maybe it just dissolves quickly. Since aspirin is a parity product, all aspirin is the same and therefore functions the same.

Works Like Anything Else

12   If you don't find the word *acts* in an ad, you will probably find the weasel word *works*. In fact, the two words are almost interchangeable in advertising. Watch out for ads that say a product "works against," "works like," "works for," or "works longer." As with *acts*, *works* is the same meaningless verb used to make you think that this product really does something, and maybe even something special or unique. But *works*, like *acts*, is basically a word empty of any specific meaning.

Like Magic

13   Whenever advertisers want you to stop thinking about the product and start thinking about something bigger, better, or more attractive than the product, they use that very popular weasel word *like*. The word *like* is the advertiser's equivalent of a magician's use of misdirection. *Like* gets you to ignore the product and concentrate on the claim the advertiser

is making about it. "For skin like peaches and cream" claims the ad for a skin cream. What is this ad really claiming? It doesn't say this cream will give you peaches-and-cream skin. There is no verb in this claim, so it doesn't even mention using the product. How is skin ever like "peaches and cream"? Remember, ads must be read literally and exactly, according to the dictionary definition of words. (Remember *virtually* in the Eli Lilly case.) The ad is making absolutely no promise or claim whatsoever for this skin cream. If you think this cream will give you soft, smooth, youthful-looking skin, you are the one who has read that meaning into the ad.

14 The wine that claims "It's like taking a trip to France" wants you to think about a romantic evening in Paris as you walk along the boulevard after a wonderful meal in an intimate little bistro. Of course, you don't really believe that a wine can take you to France, but the goal of the ad is to get you to think pleasant, romantic thoughts about France and not about how the wine tastes or how expensive it may be. That little word *like* has taken you away from crushed grapes into a world of your own imaginative making. Who knows, maybe the next time you buy wine, you'll think those pleasant thoughts when you see this brand of wine, and you'll buy it. Or, maybe you weren't even thinking about buying wine at all, but now you just might pick up a bottle the next time you're shopping. Ah, the power of *like* in advertising.

15 How about the most famous "like" claim of all, "**Winston**[3] tastes good like a cigarette should"? Ignoring the grammatical error here, you might want to know what this claim is saying. Whether a cigarette tastes good or bad is a subjective judgment because what tastes good to one person may well taste horrible to another. There are many people who say all cigarettes taste terrible, other people who say only some cigarettes taste all right, and still others who say all cigarettes taste good. Who's right? Everyone, because taste is a matter of personal judgment.

16 Moreover, note the use of the conditional, *should*. The complete claim is, "Winston tastes good like a cigarette should taste." But should cigarettes taste good? Again, this is a matter of personal judgment and probably depends most on one's experiences with smoking. So, the Winston ad is simply saying that Winston cigarettes are just like any other cigarette: Some people like them and some people don't. On that statement **R. J. Reynolds**[4] conducted a very successful multimillion-dollar advertising campaign that helped keep Winston the number-two-selling cigarette in the United States, close behind number one, Marlboro.

Can It Be Up to the Claim?

17 Analyzing ads for doublespeak requires that you pay attention to every word in the ad and determine what each word really means. Advertisers try to wrap their claims in language that sounds concrete, specific, and objective, when in fact the language of advertising is anything but. Your job is to read carefully and listen critically so that when the announcer says that "**Crest**[5] can be of significant value...," you know immediately that this claim says

absolutely nothing. Where is the doublespeak in this ad? Start with the second word.

18   Once again, you have to look at what words really mean, not what you think they mean or what the advertiser wants you to think they mean. The ad for Crest only says that using Crest "can be" of "significant value." What really throws you off in this ad is the brilliant use of *significant*. It draws your attention to the word *value* and makes you forget that the ad only claims that Crest "can be." The ad doesn't say that Crest *is* of value, only that it is "able" or "possible" to be of value, because that's all that *can* means.

19   It's so easy to miss the importance of those little words, *can be*. Almost as easy as missing the importance of the words *up to* in an ad. These words are very popular in sale ads. You know, the ones that say "Up to 50 percent Off!" Now, what does that claim mean? Not much, because the store or manufacturer has to reduce the price of only a few items by 50 percent. Everything else can be reduced a lot less, or not even reduced. Moreover, don't you want to know 50 percent off of what? Is it 50 percent off the "manufacturer's suggested list price," which is the highest possible price? Was the price artificially inflated and then reduced? In other ads, *up to* expresses an ideal situation. The medicine that works "up to ten times faster," the battery that lasts "up to twice as long," and the soap that gets you "up to twice as clean," all are based on ideal situations for using those products, situations in which you can be sure you will never find yourself.

Notes

① **William Lutz**   has become nationally known for his analyses of language in advertisements and other public statements. A professor of English at Rutgers University, Lutz is former chair of the Committee on Public Doublespeak of the National Council of Teachers of English and former editor of the *Quarterly Review of Doublespeak*. His books are *Beyond Nineteen Eighty-Four* (1984), *Doublespeak From "Revenue Enhancement" to "Terminal Living": How Government, Business, Advertisers, and Others Use Language to Deceive* (1990), *The New Doublespeak: Why No One Knows What Anyone's Saying Anymore* (1997), and *Doublespeak Defined: Cut Through the Bull and Get the Point* (1999). This essay is from *Doublespeak Defined: Cut Through the Bull and Get the Point* (1999).

② **FTC**   Federal Trade Commission, 美国联邦贸易委员会

③ **Winston**   a brand of cigarette, 一种香烟牌子

④ **R. J. Reynolds**   R. J. Reynolds Tobacco Company, 美国一家烟草公司

⑤ **Crest**   a brand of toothpaste, 一种牙膏品牌

Unit Three

Exercises

Choose the correct answer to each of the following questions.

1. According to the text, the advertisers _____.
   A. cannot make whatever claims they want for the products they advertise
   B. can make claims for the products they sell in non-legal ways
   C. can find ways to avoid the law in advertising their products
   D. can make whatever claims they want for the products they advertise

2. One can infer from the text that many words advertisers use in describing the products are _____.
   A. beautiful   B. simple   C. ambiguous   D. exact

3. The word "doublespeak" in the first sentence of Paragraph 3 means _____.
   A. speaking falsely
   B. speaking in two ways
   C. speaking correctly
   D. speaking forcefully

4. The word "parity" in line 7, Paragraph 1 is close in meaning to _____.
   A. inequality   B. similarity   C. resemblance   D. equivalence

5. Which of the following statements is true?
   A. The weasel word "help" implies "solve."
   B. The weasel word "help" means "overcome."
   C. The weasel word "help" refers to "stop."
   D. The weasel word "help" only connotes "aid or assist."

6. The powerful weasel word "virtually" means _____.
   A. really
   B. actually
   C. fully
   D. in essence, though not in fact

7. The author identifies some weasel words in advertisements with the purpose of _____.
   A. criticizing the advertising industry
   B. exposing the fraudulent behaviors of some advertisers
   C. showing the real meaning of those weasel words to readers
   D. suing some of the advertisers

8. One way to analyze ads with doublespeak content is _____.
   A. to look each word up in the dictionary
   B. to ask the advertisers what their language means
   C. to read the ads several times in order to understand the meaning
   D. to read carefully and listen critically so as to determine what each word really means

9. The magic power of the claim "it's like a trip to France" lies in the fact _____.

   A. that you will go to France after tasting this wine

   B. that this wine makes you imagine a trip to France

   C. that this wine makes you think pleasantly about France

   D. that you will buy this brand of wine next time

10. Reading from the context, one can know that many people _____.

    A. have acquired the ability to read ads critically

    B. may easily believe weasel words in ads

    C. pay no attention to ads

    D. do not believe in ads

On-the-job Writing: Business Memos

A memo, short for "memorandum," is a common form of communication within a business or an organization. Memos are slightly more informal than business letters, and they may be addressed to more than one person (a committee, a sales staff, an advisory board, etc.). Memos may be sent up or down the chain of command at a particular workplace, or they may be distributed laterally (横向的), across a department or between offices. Although the format of the paper memo may vary slightly from organization to organization, it often appears arranged in this manner:

TO: Editorial Staff
FROM: Louise Presaria, Editor-in-Chief. *LP*
DATE: April 22, 2016
RE: Silver Eagle Award Banquet

Because the current snowstorm is presenting problems with public transportation and also with heating outages in our building, the annual Silver Eagle Banquet originally scheduled for tomorrow night has been postponed for one week. It is now rescheduled for Thursday, April 29, beginning at 7:30 PM, in the Whitaker conference room.

I look forward to seeing you all there. Each of you has done a marvelous job this year and greatly deserves to share the benefits that come with our industry's most prestigious award.

Note that the name of the sender is usually accompanied by the sender's handwritten initials, rather than a full signature as in a business letter. Also, in some memos, the term "Re" ("in reference to") may be substituted for the word "Subject."

Many memos are brief, containing important bulletins (公告，告示), announcements, or reminders, as illustrated in this sample.

Other in-house (机构内部的) memos — those explaining policies or procedures, for example — may be long and complex. Lengthy memos may begin with a summary or statement of general purpose and may use headings (such as "Background Information," "Previous Action," or "Recommendations") to identify various parts of the discussion.

All business memos, regardless of length, share a common goal: the clear, concise communication of useful information from writer to reader.

Unit Four

Text A

Pre-reading Activities

1. Read the title of the article and describe some characteristics of "a difficult boss."
2. In your own work experience, what kinds of bosses have you met?
3. What is the most important thing in the workplace—professional knowledge or communication skills? What other knowledge or skills might be important?

How to Deal with a Difficult Boss
Donna Brown Hogarty

1. Bad bosses often have a recognizable **modus operandi**①. Harry Levinson, a management psychologist in Waltham, **Massachusetts**②, has catalogued problem bosses, from the bully to the **jellyfish**③ to the disapproving perfectionist. If you're suffering from a bad boss, chances are he or she combines several of these traits and can be dealt with effectively if you use the right strategy.

2. **The Bully.** During his first week on the job, a new account manager at a small **Pennsylvania** advertising agency agreed to return some materials to a client. When he mentioned this at a staff meeting, the boss turned beet red, his lips began to quiver, and he shouted that the new employee should call his client and confess he didn't know anything about the advertising business and would not be returning the materials.

3. Over the next few months, as the account manager watched coworkers cower under the boss's browbeating, he realized that the tyrant fed on fear. Employees who tried the hardest to avoid his ire were most likely to catch it. "He was like a schoolyard bully," the manager recalls, "and I've known since childhood that, when confronted, most bullies back down."

4. Armed with newfound confidence and growing knowledge of the ad business, he matched his boss's behavior. "If he raised his voice, I'd raise mine," the manager recalls. True to type, the boss started to treat him with grudging respect. Eventually, the young man moved up the ranks and was rarely subjected to his boss's outbursts.

5. Although standing up to the bully often works, it could make matters worse. Mardy

Grothe recommends a different strategy: reasoning with him after he's calmed down. "Some bosses have had a problem with temper control all their lives and are not pleased with this aspect of their personality," he explains. Want a **litmus test**[4]? If the boss attempts to compensate for an outburst by overreacting and trying to "make nice" the next day, says Grothe, he or she feels guilty about yesterday's behavior.

6   Grothe suggests explaining to your boss how his temper affects you. For instance, you might say, "I know you're trying to improve my performance, but yelling makes me less productive because it upsets me."

7   Whatever strategy you choose, deal with the bully as soon as possible, because "once a dominant/subservient relationship is established, it becomes difficult to loosen," warns industrial psychologist James Fisher. Fisher also suggests confronting your boss behind closed doors whenever possible, to avoid being disrespectful. If your boss continues to be overbearing, try these strategies from psychologist Leonard Felder, author of *Does Someone at Work Treat You Badly?*

- To keep your composure while the boss is screaming, repeat a calming phrase to yourself, such as "Ignore the anger. It isn't yours."
- Focus on a humorous aspect of your boss's appearance. If she's got a double chin, watch her flesh shake while she's yammering. "By realizing that even the most intimidating people are vulnerable, you can more easily relax," explains Felder.
- Wait for your boss to take a breath. Then try this **comeback line**[5]: "I want to hear what you're saying. You've got to slow down."
- Finally, never relax with an abusive boss, no matter how charming he or she can be, says Stanley Bing. "The bully will worm his or her way into your heart **as a way of positioning your face under his foot.**[6]"

8   **The Workaholic.** "Some bosses don't know the difference between work and play," says Nancy Ahlrichs, vice president of client services at the Indianapolis office of Right Associates, an international **outplacement firm**[7]. "If you want to reach them at night or on a Saturday, just call the office." Worse, such a boss invades your every waking hour, making it all but impossible to separate your own home life from the office.

9   Ahlrichs advises setting limits on your availability. Make sure the boss knows you can be reached in a crisis, but as a matter of practice go home at a set time. If he responds angrily, reassure him that you will tackle any project first thing in the morning. Get him to set the priorities, so you can decide which tasks can wait.

10   If you have good rapport with the boss, says Mardy Grothe, consider discussing the problem openly. Your goal is to convince him that just as he needs to meet deadlines, you have personal responsibilities that are equally important.

11   **The Jellyfish.** "My boss hires people with the assumption that we all know our jobs,"

says a woman who works for a small firm in **New England**. "Unfortunately, he hates conflict. If someone makes a mistake, we have to tiptoe around instead of moving to correct it, so we don't hurt anyone's feelings."

12　　Her boss is a jellyfish. He has refused to establish even a basic **pecking order**® in his office. As a result, a secretary sat on important correspondence for over a month, risking a client's **tax write-offs**⑨. Because no one supervises the firm's support staff, the secretary never received a reprimand, and nobody was able to prevent such mishaps from recurring. The jellyfish simply can't take charge because he's afraid of creating conflicts.

13　　So "you must take charge," suggests Lee Colby, a **Minneapolis**-based management consultant. "Tell the jellyfish: 'This is what I think I ought to be doing. What do you think?' You are taking the first step, without stepping on your boss's toes."

14　　Building an indecisive supervisor's confidence is another good strategy. For example, if you can supply hard facts and figures, you can then use them to justify any course you recommend—and gently ease the jellyfish into taking a firmer position.

15　　**The Perfectionist.** When Nancy Ahlrichs was fresh out of college, she landed her first full-time job, supervising the advertising design and layout of a small-town newspaper. On deadline day, the paper's irritable general manager would suddenly appear over her shoulder, inspecting her work for errors. Then he'd ask a barrage of questions, ending with the one Ahlrichs dreaded most: "Are you sure you'll make the deadline?"

16　　"I never missed a single deadline," Ahlrichs says, "yet every week he'd ask the same question. I felt belittled by his lack of confidence in me."

17　　Ironically, the general manager was lowering the staff's productivity. To paraphrase **Voltaire**®, the perfect is the enemy of the good. According to psychiatrist Allan Mallinger, co-author with Jeannette DeWyze of *Too Perfect: When Being in Control Gets Out of Control*, "the perfectionist's over-concern for thoroughness slows down everyone's work. When everything has to be done perfectly, tasks loom larger." The nit-picking boss who is behind schedule becomes even more difficult, making subordinates ever more miserable.

18　　"Remember," says Leonard Felder, "the perfectionist needs to find something to worry about." To improve your lot with a perfectionist boss, get her to focus on the big picture. If she demands that you redo a task you've just completed, mention your other assignments and ask her to prioritize. Often, a boss will let the work you've completed stand—especially when she realizes another project may be put on hold. If your boss is nervous about a particular project, offer regular reports. By keeping the perfectionist posted, you might circumvent constant supervision.

19　　Finally, protect yourself emotionally. "You can't depend on the perfectionist for encouragement," says Mallinger. "You owe it to yourself to get a second opinion of your work by asking others."

20   **The Aloof Boss.** When Gene Bergoffen, now **CEO**[11] of the National Private Truck Council, worked for another trade association and asked to be included in the decision-making process, his boss was brusque and inattentive. The boss made decisions alone, and very quickly. "We used to call him '**Ready, Fire, Aim**[12],'" says Bergoffen.

21   Many workers feel frozen out by their boss in subtle ways. Perhaps he doesn't invite them to key meetings or he might never be available to discuss projects. "At the core of every good boss is the ability to communicate expectations clearly," says Gerard Roche, chairman of Heidrick & Struggles, an executive search firm. "Employees should never have to wonder what's on a boss's mind."

22   If your boss fails to give you direction, Roche says, "the worst thing you can do is nothing. Determine the best course of action, then say to your boss: 'Unless I hear otherwise, here's what I'm going to do.'"

23   Other strategies: When your boss does not invite you to meetings or include you in decision making, speak up. "Tell her you have information that might prove to be valuable," suggests Lee Colby. If that approach doesn't work, find an intermediary who respects your work and can persuade the boss to listen to your views.

24   To understand your boss's inability to communicate, it's vital to examine his work style. "Some like hard data, logically arranged in writing," says Colby. "Others prefer face-to-face meetings. Find out what makes your boss tick—and speak in his or her language."

25   Understanding your boss can make your job more bearable in a number of ways. For instance, try offering the boss two solutions to a problem—one that will make him happy, and one that will help you to reach your goals. Even the most difficult boss will usually allow you to solve problems in your own way—as long as he's convinced of your loyalty to him.

26   No matter which type of bad boss you have, think twice before going over his head. Try forming a committee with your colleagues and approaching the boss all together. The difficult boss is usually unaware of the problem and often is eager to make amends.

27   Before embarking on any course of action, engage in some self-analysis. Chances are, no matter how difficult your boss is, you are also contributing to the conflict. "Talk to people who know you both, and get some honest feedback," suggests Mardy Grothe. "If you can fix the ways in which you're contributing to the problem, you'll be more likely to get your boss to change."

28   Even if you can't, there's a **silver lining:**[13] the worst bosses often have the most to teach you. Bullies, for example, are frequently masters at reaching difficult goals. Perfectionists can often prod you into exceeding your own expectations.

29   As a young resident psychologist at the Menninger psychiatric hospital in Topeka, **Kansas**, Harry Levinson was initially overwhelmed by the high standards of founder Karl

Menninger. "I felt I was never going to be able to diagnose patients as well as he did or perform to such high academic requirements," Levinson recalls. He even considered quitting. But in the end, he rose to the challenge, and today he believes he owes much of his success to what he learned during that critical period.

30　　Dealing with a difficult boss forces you to set priorities, to overcome fears, to stay calm under the gun, and to negotiate for better working conditions. And the skills you sharpen to ease a tense relationship will stand you in good stead throughout your career. "Employees who are able to survive a trying boss often earn the respect of higher-ups for their ability to manage a situation," says Levinson. "And because a difficult boss can cause rapid turnover, those who stick it out often advance quickly."

31　　Your bad boss can also teach you what not to do with subordinates as you move up—and one day enable you to be a better boss yourself.

Notes

① **modus operandi**　It is a Latin phrase, approximately translated as *method or mode of operating*. It refers to someone's habits of working, particularly in the context of business or criminal investigations, but also more generally. 做法，惯技

② **Massachusetts**　New England eastern seaboard state. Boston is its capital. 马萨诸塞州；麻省（美国东北部一州，首府波士顿；是清教徒先辈移民首次登陆美洲的地方，也是美国最初成立的13个州之一，以哈佛大学和麻省理工学院等名牌大学而闻名）

　Pennsylvania　state in the eastern United States, south of New York state. Philadelphia is its capital. 宾夕法尼亚州（美国东北部一州，是美国最初成立的13个州之一，也是美国独立战争期间美国人民争取从英国人手中获得独立的重要战斗中心。以出产大量钢铁和煤闻名）

　Indianapolis　capital of Indiana, state in the Midwest region of the United States, 印第安纳波利斯（美国中西部以农业著称的印第安纳州的首府）

　New England　the six states of Maine, Vermont, New Hampshire, Connecticut, Rhode Island, and Massachusetts in the northeastern United States, 新英格兰（指美国东北部各州，包括缅因州、新罕布什尔州、佛蒙特州、马萨诸塞州、罗得岛州及康涅狄格州。因17世纪包括"五月花"号船到达美洲的英国人在内的早期移民开始在此定居而得名）

　Minneapolis　capital of Minnesota, state in the upper Midwest tier of the United States, 明尼阿波利斯，明尼苏达州（美国北部一州，为工业区和农业区，兼有许多奶牛场）首府

② **Kansas**　Great Plains state in the central United States, 堪萨斯州（美国中部大平原上一州，尤以出产大量小麦闻名）

③ **jellyfish**　a person lacking backbone or firmness, 软蛋；没骨气的人

④ **litmus**　a chemical that turns red when it touches acid and blue when it touches an alkali, 石蕊；A **litmus test** is an indicator which suggests or predicts a broader course of action or set of circumstances. 试金石

Unit Four

⑤ **comeback line**   a sharp and witty reply, 机智的回答
⑥ **as a way of positioning your face under his foot**   as a way of gaining control over you, 作为一种欺压你的方式
⑦ **outplacement firm**   a firm that provides company assistance in finding new jobs for terminated workers of the company, 新职介绍公司
⑧ **pecking order**   social hierarchy, 社会等级
⑨ **tax write-offs**   tax credit for work-related expenses, 税金减免
⑩ **Voltaire** (1694—1778)   French Enlightenment philosopher, 伏尔泰, 法国作家和哲学家, 启蒙运动的领导人之一。他的思想曾对法国大革命产生了影响。他最著名的作品是小说《老实人》。
⑪ **CEO**   chief executive officer (the highest-ranking person in a business), (公司) 首席行政长官; 总裁
⑫ **"Ready, Fire, Aim"**   the usual order would be "Ready, Aim, Fire." By using the phrase in its present order, Bergoffen and his colleagues show their disapproval of their boss who does not communicate well with his people and thus leaves them wondering why he is doing, what he is doing and what is expected of them.
⑬ **silver lining**   a hopeful prospect. It is part of the phrase "Every cloud has a silver lining." 困难中看到的光明

Vocabulary

1. sitcom [ˈsɪtkɒm] *n.* on television or radio, a comedy series in which the same characters appear in different situations each week, 情景喜剧
2. catalogue [ˈkæt(ə)lɒg] *vt.* to record something, especially in a list, 将……列入目录
3. trait [treɪt; treɪ] *n.* a personality characteristic, (某人性格中的) 特性, 品质
4. beet [biːt] *n.* a vegetable with a round dark red root, 甜菜块根
5. quiver [ˈkwɪvə] *vi.* to tremble because of cold or emotional upset, 颤抖, 发抖
6. cower [ˈkaʊə] *vi.* to bend low and move back out of fear, cringe, 畏缩
7. browbeat [ˈbraʊbiːt] *v.* to force someone to do something, especially in a threatening way, 对……吹胡子瞪眼睛, 吓唬
8. tyrant [ˈtaɪrənt] *n.* a ruler who uses power cruelly or unfairly, 暴君似的人; 专横的人
9. ire [ˈaɪə] *n.* anger, 愤怒
10. confront [kənˈfrʌnt] *vt.* to meet face to face in an angy or defiant manner, 勇敢地面对, 对抗
11. grudging [ˈgrʌdʒɪŋ] *adj.* given or done in an unwilling way, 勉强的; 不情愿的
12. outburst [ˈaʊtbɜːst] *n.* a sudden, violent burst of emotions, (感情的) 突然爆发
13. personality [pɜːsəˈnælɪtɪ] *n.* character, especially as shown in interactions with others, 个性, 性格
14. dominant [ˈdɒmɪnənt] *adj.* most powerful; controlling, 统治的, 支配的
15. subservient [səbˈsɜːvɪənt] *adj.* obedient; accepting a lower position, 从属的; 恭顺的

16. overbearing [ˌəʊvəˈbeərɪŋ] *adj.* always trying to control other people without considering their wishes or feelings, 傲慢的；专横的
17. composure [kəmˈpəʊʒə] *n.* calmness and control, poise, 冷静，镇定
18. yammer [ˈjæmə] *vi. informal* to talk continuously in an annoying way, 吼叫，大声地说
19. intimidating [ɪnˈtɪmɪdeɪtɪŋ] *adj.* threatening, inspiring fear, 令人紧张不安的
20. vulnerable [ˈvʌlnərəbl] *adj.* easily harmed or hurt, 脆弱的，易受伤的
21. abusive [əˈbjuːsɪv] *adj.* rude and cruel, harmful to the physical or emotional wellbeing of another, 谩骂的
22. tackle [ˈtæk(ə)l] *vt.* to take on a difficult problem, 处理，对付
23. priority [praɪˈɒrɪtɪ] *n.* position of first importance, 优先考虑的事
24. reprimand [ˈreprɪmɑːnd] *n.* rebuke, strong statement of reproof, usually directed at a subordinate, 申斥，谴责
25. mishap [ˈmɪshæp] *n.* bad luck or an unlucky event or accident, 不幸的事，灾祸
26. recur [rɪˈkɜː] *vi.* to happen again, 再次发生
27. barrage [ˈbærɑːʒ] *n.* an outpouring of criticism, questions, complaints that are said at the same time or very quickly one after another, 连珠炮似的问题、批评
28. dread [dred] *vt.* to anticipate with anxiety and reluctance, 担心，畏惧
29. belittle [bɪˈlɪt(ə)l] *vt.* to make seem small or unimportant, 轻视
30. paraphrase [ˈpærəfreɪz] *vt.* to express in a shorter, clearer, or different way what someone has said or written, 意译，改述
31. psychiatrist [saɪˈkaɪətrɪst] *n.* a doctor trained in the treatment of mental illness, 精神病医生
32. nitpicking [ˈnɪtˌpɪkɪŋ] *adj. informal* arguing about small unimportant details or trying to find small mistakes, 挑剔，吹毛求疵
33. subordinate [səˈbɔːdɪnət] *n.* someone who has a lower position and less authority, underling, 部下，下级
34. circumvent [sɜːkəmˈvent] *vt.* to avoid or bypass, especially cleverly or illegally, 回避，规避
35. brusque [brʊsk; bruːsk] *adj.* blunt and rude in manner or speech, 莽撞的，粗鲁的
36. subtle [ˈsʌt(ə)l] *adj.* hard to detect; behaving in a skillful and clever way, especially using indirect methods or language, 微妙的，巧妙的
37. intermediary [ˌɪntəˈmiːdɪərɪ] *n.* someone who carries messages between people who are unwilling or unable to meet, go-between, 中间人
38. prod [prɒd] *v.* to goad into action, especially when the subject is lazy or unwilling, 敦促，激励
39. exceed [ɪkˈsiːd; ek-] *vt.* to go beyond, to be greater than, 超过，超出
40. resident [ˈrezɪdənt] *adj.* [*only before noun*] living or working in a particular place or institution, （在某机构）居住（工作）的
41. turnover [ˈtɜːnəʊvə] *n.* the rate at which people leave an organization and are replaced by others, 人员流动率
42. advance [ədˈvɑːns] *vi.* to rise in rank, position, or importance, 升迁

Unit Four

Useful Expressions

1. **feed on:** to use something in order to continue to exist or become stronger
   (1) Both sides in the conflict feed on old suspicions.
   (2) Prejudice feeds on ignorance.
2. **back down:** to admit that one is wrong or that one has lost an argument
   (1) Both sides have refused to back down.
   (2) We could see that he would back down if we stood firm.
3. **true to type / form:** behaving in an expected manner
   (1) True to form, Henry turned up late.
   (2) When that sort of person cheats at cards, I am not at all surprised—they're just acting true to type.
4. **move up:** to get a better job in a company or advance to a higher rank
   (1) To move up, you'll need the right training.
   (2) He moved up to become publishing director and editor-in-chief.
5. **be subjected to:** to be forced to experience something very unpleasant, especially over a long time
   (1) All our products are subjected to rigorous testing.
   (2) These prisoners were taken to places where they would be subjected to interrogation through torture.
6. **stand up to:** to refuse to accept unfair treatment from a person or organization
   (1) He'll respect you more if you stand up to him.
   (2) The British official tells people to stand up to terrorism.
7. **behind closed doors:** in private, not open to public observation
   (1) It seems that the deal was made behind closed doors.
   (2) Football authorities ordered the club to play its next two games behind closed doors after the riots in February.
8. **worm your way into somebody's heart /affections/confidence:** to subtly earn someone's love or trust
   (1) He tried to worm his way into her heart as a friend.
   (2) She was confident she could worm her way into their affections.
9. **sit on:** (*informal*) to delay dealing with something
   (1) I sent my application about six weeks ago and they've just been sitting on it.
   (2) Are these people still sitting on your letter? It's time you had a reply!
10. **step on one's toes:** (*American English*) to offend someone, especially by intruding on that person's responsibilities
    (1) If you criticize someone's job performance, you may step on his or her toes.
    (2) Mind you, don't go stepping on father's toes again by mentioning his trouble at work.

11. **put on hold:** to put aside to deal with at a later time
    (1) Since having the kids, my career has been put on hold.
    (2) Plans to sell genetically modified wheat in the U.S. have been put on hold by Monsanto, the agrobiotech giant in St Louis, Missouri.
12. **keep posted:** to regularly tell someone the most recent news about something
    (1) I'll keep you posted on his progress.
    (2) Mr. Hopkins, I want you to keep me posted on whatever happens while I'm off the job.
13. **freeze out:** to deliberately prevent someone from being involved in something, to exclude
    (1) Other traders did everything they could to freeze us out of the business.
    (2) Give consumers the option to freeze out credit crooks.
14. **at the core of:** at the most important or central part of something
    (1) Debt is at the core of the problem.
    (2) He has been at the core of some of the darkest activities in this country over the last four years.
15. **think twice before doing:** to very carefully consider the dangers or problems before deciding to do something
    (1) I'd think twice before taking out such a large loan.
    (2) Parents should think twice before making their backyard an extreme sports zone.
16. **make amends:** to do something conciliatory to show regret for hurting or upsetting someone
    (1) He seized the chance to make amends for his behavior.
    (2) He should find a way to make amends to the surviving relatives both in word and deed.
17. **embark on / upon:** to start something, especially something new, difficult, or exciting
    (1) He embarked on a new career as a teacher.
    (2) I should have thought twice before I embarked on such a hazardous project as that.
18. **rise to the challenge:** to act in response to a difficult situation and be successful
    (1) I've no doubt that Britain will continue to rise to the challenges ahead, so this country will remain in the spotlight throughout the coming century.
    (2) These can make a person either rise to the challenge or let it get the best of them.
19. **stand / serve / hold in good stead:** to be very useful in the future
    (1) His years of training were standing him in good stead.
    (2) He said that lessons learned from their World Cup final defeat by Australia would stand them in good stead for the future.
20. **stick it out:** to continue doing something that is difficult, painful, or boring
    (1) It wasn't a happy period of his life, but he stuck it out.
    (2) "I only wish people would see that more because he's had a very hard time and yet he's stuck it out, and he's still very positive." (Prince William on his father, Prince Charles)

Unit Four

Understanding the text

1. In giving suggestions on how to deal with the bully boss, the author advises us never to relax with an abusive boss. Why?
2. Will going home at a set time be a good way to separate your personal life and work?
3. What will be the best way to deal with a jellyfish boss?
4. To avoid constant supervision from the perfectionist, what do you need to do?
5. When your boss does not include you in the decision-making process, what can you do?
6. What are the author's general suggestions for dealing with all types of difficult bosses?
7. Hogarty claims that "the worst bosses often have the most to teach you" (Paragraph 28). What examples does she give to support that point? Have you ever had a bad boss from whom you learned something? If so, what did you learn and how did you learn it?
8. In general, is Hogarty's tone in discussing how to deal with difficult bosses pessimistic or optimistic? What specific details support your answer?

Exercises

A. Fill in the blanks with the appropriate words from the text.

1. _____ newfound confidence and growing knowledge of the ad business, he _____ his boss's behavior. "If he raised his voice, I'd raise mine," the manager recalls. _____, the boss started to treat him with _____. Eventually, the young man moved up the ranks and was rarely _____ his boss's outbursts. (Paragraph 4)

2. _____ strategy you choose, deal with the bully as soon as possible, because "_____ a dominant/subservient relationship is _____, it becomes difficult to loosen," _____ industrial psychologist James Fisher. Fisher also suggests _____ your boss behind closed doors whenever possible, to avoid being disrespectful. (Paragraph 7)

3. Ahlrichs advises _____ your availability. Make sure the boss knows you can be _____ in a crisis, but as a matter of practice go home _____ a _____ time. If he responds angrily, reassure him that you will tackle any project _____ thing in the _____. Get him to _____ the priorities, so you can decide which tasks can wait. (Paragraph 9)

4. When Nancy Ahlrichs was _____ out of college, she _____ her first full-time job, supervising the advertising design and layout of a small-town newspaper. On _____, the paper's irritable general manager would suddenly appear _____ her shoulder,

inspecting her work for errors. Then he'd ask _____ of questions, ending with the one Ahlrichs dreaded most: "Are you sure you'll _____?" (Paragraph 15)

5. "I never _____ a single deadline," Ahlrichs says, "yet every week he'd ask the same question. I felt belittled by his lack of confidence _____ me." (Paragraph 16)

6. Many workers feel _____ by their boss in _____ ways. Perhaps he doesn't invite them to _____ meetings or he might never be _____ to discuss projects. "___ the _____ of every good boss is the ability to _____ expectations clearly," says Gerard Roche, chairman of Heidrick & Struggles, an executive search firm. "Employees should never have to wonder what's _____ a boss's _____." (Paragraph 21)

7. Before _____ any course of action, _____ some self-analysis. _____, no matter how difficult your boss is, you are also _____ the conflict. "Talk to people who know you both, and get some honest feedback," suggests Mardy Grothe. "If you can fix the ways in which you're _____ the problem, you'll be more likely to get your boss to change." (Paragraph 27)

B. Choose from the words given below to complete the following sentences, changing the word form where necessary.

abusive	confront	dominant	exceed
circumvent	recall	dread	match
priority	subtle	tackle	vulnerable

1. Their constant arguments left her feeling increasingly _____ and insecure.
2. I _____ having to meet his parents.
3. I seem to _____ I've met him before somewhere.
4. I detected a _____ change in his attitude towards us.
5. Few cities in Europe can _____ the cultural richness of Berlin.
6. Advertising restrictions _____ easily _____.
7. The issue of climate change was the _____ theme of the conference.
8. He was apparently _____ to the flight attendants because they refused to serve him alcohol.
9. He would have liked to be able to _____ and examine his own previous self.
10. Health insurance will be our top _____.
11. You will need to fill in a form for any claim _____ £500.
12. There are many ways of _____ this problem.

Unit Four

C. Fill in the blanks with the phrases given below, changing the form where necessary.

back down	be subjected to	stand up to
embark upon	move up	step on one's toes
feed on	compensate for	put on hold
freeze out	sit on	stick it out

1. The Government's record _____ scrutiny in the weeks before the election.
2. He _____ to the position of manager.
3. Eventually, Roberto _____ and apologized.
4. They _____ my application for over a month now.
5. This payment more than _____ what we've lost.
6. He wasn't afraid to _____ bullies.
7. I know things are difficult at the moment, but if we just _____, I'm sure everything will be OK in the end.
8. He _____ of official life.
9. We _____ a new project later this year.
10. Since having the kids, my career _____.
11. We have an understanding: I don't _____, she doesn't step on mine.
12. The singer _____ admiration from the public.

D. Fill in the blanks with the expressions given below, changing the form where necessary.

at the core of	land (a job)
behind schedule	loom large
chances are	meet the deadline
first thing (in the morning)	rise to the challenge
have good rapport with	think twice

1. I'd _____ before buying that car if I were you.
2. He _____ just _____ a senior editorial job with a men's magazine.
3. _____ that they'll be late anyway.
4. It's not an easy task, but I'm sure John _____.
5. The issue of pay _____ at this Easter's teacher conference.
6. She _____ her staff.
7. Financial instability lies _____ the institute's problems.
8. He said he'd phone back _____ tomorrow.
9. The research project is already two years _____.
10. If we can't _____, they won't give us another contract.

E. Read the following text and choose the best word for each blank from the choices given.

    Successfully managing a difficult boss is a challenge but often feasible. First, you should try to understand the reasons for your boss's difficult behavior. (1) _____ your boss generally behaves in a fairly reasonable manner, and that his/her difficult behavior seems to be a (2) _____ of stress overload rather than his/her character, (3) _____ are that the behavior can be modified. If your boss's behavior seems to reflect a chronically hostile, (4) _____ style of interacting regardless of the amount of stress in the worksite, the chances are less positive (5) _____ the behavior can change. In fact, you may want to consider (6) _____ counsel from a trusted mentor or human resources professional to evaluate your options. Second, you have to manage your own (7) _____ emotions regarding his/her behavior so that you do not (8) _____ self-defeating behavior (e.g., stonewalling, or counter-attacking your boss). Third, once you understand and have managed your own negative reactions, you may work to (9) _____ your issues/concerns—but framed in a helpful positive manner—creating an atmosphere for problem (10) _____ .

1. A. Assume   B. Assumption   C. Assuming   D. Assumed
2. A. reason   B. matter   C. result   D. factor
3. A. facts   B. chances   C. cases   D. conditions
4. A. abuse   B. abusing   C. abusive   D. abused
5. A. that   B. what   C. such   D. so
6. A. avoiding   B. searching   C. seeking   D. looking
7. A. positive   B. negative   C. overwhelming   D. profound
8. A. engage in   B. take in   C. involve in   D. live in
9. A. conduct   B. communicate   C. conceal   D. commit
10. A. solution   B. resolution   C. salvation   D. revolution

F. Translate the following sentences into English, using the phrases and expressions given in parentheses.

1. 公司一直搁置他的报告。(sit on)
2. 她是不是学习方法不对头？(have a problem with)
3. 你必须为你的侮辱行为向他们赔礼道歉。(make amends)
4. 英语老师就是没法使他相信学英语的重要性。(convince...of...)
5. 我们不能报道讨论的内容，因为讨论是秘密进行的。(behind closed doors)
6. 现在人们总是忙着赶最后期限。(meet deadlines)
7. 他一直不断地向我提供他的消息。(keep somebody posted)
8. 在接受该提议前我本应仔细考虑，当时听起来就有点可疑。(think twice)
9. 她是刚毕业的研究生。(fresh out of)
10. 我们可以用单子来确定事情的先后顺序、计划活动并衡量进展情况。(set priorities)

Unit Four

Text B

Bad Bosses and How to Handle Them
Barbara Moses[①]

1. He goes **from strength to strength**[②], even though everyone knows he has the spine of a jellyfish. He won't lobby for the resources you need or stand up for you on critical issues. As a result, you are doing work below your own standards, but he doesn't seem to care—so long as it gets done within the budget.

2. At the first sign of a conflict, he runs. He tolerates toxic behaviour from your co-workers and perhaps even encourages petty rivalries. He is a classic example of the weak manager, and a very bad boss.

3. Bad bosses—whether jerks, bullies, or micro-managers—have always been with us. Today, however, we're seeing more bad bosses than ever before. **As a result of institutionalized leanness**[③], overextended managers are both short-tempered and too busy or ill-trained to provide staff with the support they need. No one has as much power as a bad boss to unnerve you and wreak havoc on your sense of self-esteem. This is why it is commonly said that people don't quit jobs, they quit bosses.

4. What makes for a bad boss? Some are just plain nasty, but often, **a bad boss is all in the eye of the beholder. One person's boss from hell may be another person's pinup.**[④] If you need regular direction, for example, you will be miserable with a hands-off, absentee manager, but if you have strong needs for autonomy you will flourish under the same regime.

5. Then again, the problem could be simply bad chemistry. She's an introvert and you're an extrovert. You like direction, she thinks you're "needy." You like to go home at six, she's a workaholic. So before you assume your boss is a complete jerk, ask yourself: Does she get along with others? Does she pick on everyone, or just you?

6. The key to getting on with a boss is to manage him by understanding his underlying motivations, which may be different than you think. Here are some common types of bad bosses, their motivations, and strategies for dealing with them. If you're a manager, look for yourself in these descriptions:

The weak manager

7. She won't stand up for you. She aggressively avoids taking risks. She's vague and her commitments have the sticking power of water.

8. But the underlying causes of her behaviour can vary. Often, she simply wants to be liked by everyone and can't stand conflict. It's also possible she's too busy to understand when there is a problem or too burned out to care. Frequently, such managers are reluctant

to be managers at all and would much rather be getting on with their own work as individuals.

9   They may also be ill-trained and lacking management skills.

10   If you are dealing with a weak manager, identify the problem. For example, if your manager needs to be liked by everyone, avoid communications that suggest contentious or highly charged emotional issues. Where you can, solve conflicts yourself. If her problem is that she is spineless and refuses to take on any leadership role, talk to your boss's boss.

11   If your boss is too burned out to care or is a reluctant manager, work around her. Take the initiative to set out the parameters of the work. Give yourself the feedback you need. Pin your boss down by e-mail to a suggested meeting time.

12   Make her life easy by only talking to her about critical issues. If your boss is lacking management skills, tell her what you need from her to do your job. Then cover yourself by sending an e-mail.

The political manager

13   He has an unerring ability to know what will make him look good. He will go to bat for you only on issues that serve his political agenda. He's sneaky and plays favourites. He won't think twice about using you as a sacrificial lamb to support his own career goals.

14   Support his high need for recognition by making him look good on strategic projects. Focus your own efforts on "high-value" work. Be prepared to share the limelight, even if it kills you. Don't trust him to have your own interests at heart. Pitch him on work you want to do by emphasizing its profile and importance to senior management.

The black-and-white manager

15   He just doesn't get it—either because **he has the IQ of an eraser or he is as concrete as they come**.⑤ He doesn't understand context, nuance, or high-level ideas.

16   If his problem is intellectual deficiency, indulge him like a misguided child. Better yet, ignore him if you can. But if the problem is one of cognitive style, shape your communications to his needs. If he is fact-oriented, don't waste your time painting compelling arguments based on ideas. Simply state the facts and provide information unembellished.

The obsessive micro-manager

17   She trusts you the way you'd trust a five-year-old behind the wheel of the car. No matter how much detail you give her or how many times you do and redo a piece of work, it's still not right. You're completely demotivated and have lost your sense of competence.

18   Why is she so untrusting? Is she anxious about failing to please her boss, or is she simply a control freak? If the problem is her own insecurity, anticipate issues that will make her anxious by reassuring her that you have covered all the bases. Say, for example, "In completing this I spoke to Jane Doe and took the following issues into account..." Write it

down as well, as she may be too anxious to fully process what you are saying.

The invisible manager

19 You have no one to go to for direction. She doesn't have a clue about the volume or pace of your work. You're killing yourself, but no one notices or gives you feedback.

20 This manager shares many of the underlying motivations of the weak manager. She may be invisible because she's too busy, or is a reluctant or unskilled manager.

21 If she is pressed for time, do your homework before you meet with her to make the meeting as efficient as possible. Be strategic on issues where you need support. Give yourself direction and feedback by setting milestones and regularly evaluating your effectiveness against them. Thank yourself for a job well done. Establish a mechanism for getting direction, whether it be weekly or monthly meetings at an agreed time. Hold her to her commitment.

The task master

22 He doesn't have a life, and doesn't expect you to either. You're drowning in work but he keeps heaping on more. His time-lines are ridiculous. Sometimes an extremely task-focused manager is simply shy or preoccupied, or so focused on getting the work done that he's not aware of the impact of his behaviour on the people around him. Is he aware of your work load?

23 If you've talked to him and he still doesn't get it, create your own standards for evaluating what is realistic and doable. Don't be apologetic about wanting time for a personal life. Work-life balance is your right, not a privilege. If your organization wants to "be an employer of choice," remind your boss of the incongruity between policy and behaviour.

The nasty manager

24 She's ruthless. She seems to take pleasure in watching you squirm. She has pets and you are not one of them.

25 Sometimes an apparently nasty boss is simply so task-focused that she is oblivious to how her behaviour makes you feel. Underneath a gruff exterior, as the saying goes, may be the heart of a pussycat. When you confront her, does she apologize, or get mad?

26 Regardless of what type of boss you have, your first line of defense is to speak to him, as he may not be aware of his behaviour. Don't make sweeping generalizations about his personality. Rather, talk to the specific behaviour in question and tell him how it makes you feel. You can soften your comments and avoid defensiveness by allowing your boss to save face. Introduce your statements with "You may not be aware..." or "You may not realize..." or "You may not intend..."

27 If none of these strategies work, you have two choices. If you have good personal

reasons for staying in your job—you love your work, you're learning a lot, you like the people you're working with—you can hold your nose and ignore your boss as best you can. Or, you can quit: life is too short to deal with this kind of abuse.

Notes

① **Barbara Moses** Dr. Barbara Moses is the best-selling author of *What Next? The Complete Guide to Taking Control of Your Working Life*, an international speaker, and work issues expert.

② **go from strength to strength** to have one success after another, 不断壮大

③ **As a result of institutionalized leanness** as a result of having fewer employees to do the same or more work, 由于制度化的机构精简

④ **A bad boss is all in the eye of the beholder. One person's boss from hell may be another person's pinup.** The same boss may be liked or hated by different employees, 是不是坏老板全在谁来看。一个人的魔鬼老板可能是另一个人的偶像。这两句化自两句英文谚语: "Beauty is in the eye of the beholder", 观者觉得美就是美[情人眼里出西施(对美的判断因人而异)]; "One man's meat is another man's poison": People have different perceptions of the same thing, 对甲有利的未必对乙也有利(兴趣爱好因人而异)。

⑤ **He has the IQ of an eraser or he is as concrete as they come** He has a very low IQ, or he understands definite and specific things only, not more abstract ideas.

Exercises

A. Answer the following questions on the text.

1. In Text A Donna Brown Hogarty gives five types of bad bosses while in Text B Barbara Moses lists seven types. Is there any overlap between the two lists? If the texts overlap, do the strategies to deal with the specific types of bad bosses also overlap? What are the similarities and differences? Are there contradictions? Which text is better?
2. What synonyms or related words describe each type of bad boss in the two texts?
3. Can you think of other types of bad bosses and some ways to manage them?

B. Choose the best answer to each of the following questions.

1. All of the following statements describe a typical weak manager except ____.
    A. he has the spine of a jellyfish
    B. he doesn't support his men
    C. he can't stand conflict
    D. he is not successful

2. By saying "a bad boss is all in the eye of the beholder," the author means ____.
    A. we can find bad bosses anywhere

B. the only person one sees is a bad boss

   C. one's bad boss may be another employee's good boss

   D. it all depends on the boss himself

3. To deal with a weak manager, one needs to ____.

   A. find out his manager's problem

   B. do whatever one can to finish his work

   C. tell someone above the manager

   D. tell the manager his problem

4. A political manager will do the following except ____.

   A. the thing that will make him look good

   B. the thing that will be, first and foremost, good for his employees

   C. the thing that will support his career goals

   D. the thing that will serve his political plan

5. Who is a workaholic?

   A. The political manager.

   B. The obsessive micro-manager.

   C. The task master.

   D. The nasty manager.

6. According to the author, when dealing with a bad boss, one first needs to ____.

   A. ignore the boss

   B. save the boss's face

   C. understand the boss's personality

   D. talk to the boss

On-the-job Writing: Agendas and Minutes

Both agendas and minutes need to be brief and objective.

Agendas

The written agenda focuses the purposes of the meeting and the topics you expect to cover. Even informal meetings can benefit from a written agenda, distributed ahead of time. Here are some suggestions for making an agenda:

1. Use a memo. The subject line should contain all essential information: (1) who should attend, (2) the location, (3) the day(s) of the week, (4) the complete date(s), (5) the beginning and ending times with a.m. or p.m.

2. If necessary, provide the purpose of the meeting in an opening line: *This meeting will determine the feasibility of an employees' service center.*

3. List the topics, beginning (if appropriate) with the approval of the minutes (会议纪要) of the previous meeting.

4. If it will simplify the activities of the meeting, list reports from the chair, subcommittees, or other participants. Personally alert those reporting what their time limits will be.

5. List the most important topics first, in case time runs short and some items have to be postponed.
6. Attach a detailed schedule if this is to be a multisessioned conference.
7. Attach any informational materials so participants will have time to prepare for the meeting.

Minutes of a Meeting

Organizations and committees keep official records of their meetings; such records are known as minutes. At the beginning of each meeting, those attending vote to accept the minutes from the previous meeting as prepared or to revise or clarify specific items.
The minutes of meetings should include the following information:
1. Name of the group or committee that is holding the meeting.
2. The place, time and date of the meeting.
3. The kind of meeting being held (a regular meeting or a special meeting called to discuss a specific subject or problem).
4. The number of members present. If the committee or board is small (ten or fewer), members' name should be given.
5. A statement that the person chairing the meeting and the secretary were present, or the name of the substitute if either one was absent.
6. A statement that the minutes of the previous meeting were approved or revised.
7. A list of the reports that were read and approved. It is seldom necessary to give a detailed account of the substance of the reports submitted.
8. All the main motions (or proposals) that were made, with statements as to whether they were carried, defeated, or tabled (vote postponed). Do not include motions that were withdrawn. It is also customary to include the names of those who made and seconded motions.
9. Resolutions that were adopted, written out in full. If a resolution was rejected, make a simple statement to that effect.
10. A record of all ballots, complete with the number of votes cast for and against.
11. The time that the meeting was adjourned (officially ended) and the place, time, and date of the next meeting.
12. The recording secretary's signature (and typed name) and, if desired, the signature of the person chairing the meeting.

Unit Four

Sample Meeting Agenda

JDE AND ASSOCIATES/1739 Ambar Drive/ Calabasas, CA 91360

Interdepartmental Memo

Date: July 12, 2017
To: Jack Adams, Amy Fong, Woody Rainy, Juanita Valdez, and Ben Zapolski
From: Sheila Thomes ST   818-340-6666
Director, Studio B   SThomes @ JDEassoc.com
Subject: Final Meeting on Proposal for Sheffield Gardens
Thursday, July 15, 2017, 10:00 a.m. PDT Conference Room 4

AGENDA

1. Approval of Minutes July 8, 2017, attached
2. Report from Juanita on revised test results
3. Report from Jack on section 16: bar graphs
4. Report from Sheila on printing and packaging
5. Approval of press release, attached
6. Discussion of final issues

- Delivery of documents
- Follow-through with Mr. Dolan

Please be prompt. I've arranged coffee/tea at 9:45.
Let's try to adjourn by 1 p.m.

Sample Minutes of Meetings

WARETON MEDICAL CENTER
DEPARTMENT OF MEDICINE

Minutes of the Regular Meeting of the Credentials Committee

DATE: April 18, 2018
PRESENT: M. Valden (Chairperson), R. Baron, M. Frank, J. Guern, L. Kingson, L. Kinslow (Secretary), S. Perry, B. Roman, J. Sorder, F. Sugihana

Dr. Mary Valden called the meeting to order at 8:40 p.m. The minutes of the previous meeting were unanimously approved, with the following correction: the secretary of the Department of Medicine is to be changed from Dr. Juanita Alvarez to Dr. Barbara Golden.

Old Business
None.
New Business
The request by Dr. Henry Russel for staff privileges in the Department of Medicine was discussed. Dr. James Guern made a motion that Dr. Russel be granted staff privileges. Dr. Martin Frank seconded the motion, which passed unanimously.

Similar requests by Dr. Ernest Hiram and Dr. Helen Redlands were discussed. Dr. Fred Sugihana made a motion that both physicians be granted all staff privileges except respiratory-care privileges because the two physicians had not had a sufficient number of respiratory cases. Dr. Steven Perry seconded the motion, which passed unanimously.

Dr. John Sorder and Dr. Barry Roman asked for a clarification of general duties for active staff members with respiratory-care privileges. Dr. Richard Baron stated that he would present a clarification at the next scheduled staff meeting, on May 15.

Dr. Baron asked for a volunteer to fill the existing vacancy for Emergency Room duty. Dr. Guern volunteered. He and Dr. Baron will arrange a duty schedule.

There being no further business, the meeting was adjourned at 9:15 p.m. The next regular meeting is scheduled for May 15, at 8:40 p.m.

Respectfully submitted,
Leslie Kinslow   *Mary Valden*

Leslie Kinslow   Mary Valden, M. D.
Medical Staff Secretary   Chairperson

Unit Five

Text A

Pre-reading Activities

1. Do you live with your grandparents? Do they require more attention as they get older?
2. What are your grandparents' reactions to getting older?
3. Is there any case of elder neglect around you? How do you treat your grandparents?
4. Have your grandparents ever behaved irrationally? What is your or your family's response in those situations?
5. What is your ideal of a perfect old person? What do you hope you will be like when you are sixty or seventy years old?

A Granddaughter's Fear
Natalie Angier[1]

1 I was talking business with a colleague late one afternoon when the first call came. The voice on the other end was loud and panicked; my colleague looked over at me, horrified.

2 "Natalie, is that you?" screamed my grandmother. "Natalie, I need you to do me a favor!"

3 I cupped the telephone mouthpiece. "What's wrong, Grandma?"

4 She started to cry, her voice heaving and gasping. She told me that she'd been alone since twelve o'clock—for five hours!—and that nobody was scheduled to visit her until ten that night. She couldn't stand it; she was going crazy; they'd left her all alone, and she was so afraid. She'd been calling everybody, everybody—her son (my uncle), her stepson, her grandsons. And now me.

5 "So what do you want me to do?" I muttered, although I knew the answer.

6 "Please, darling, come over! Can't you come here? Please Natalie! I'm ALL ALONE!"

7 "O.K., O.K.," I said. "I'm coming over. I'll be up there as soon as I can."

8 I hung up and told my colleague that I'd have to leave in a few minutes. But I didn't think there was any immediate crisis. My grandmother lives in an apartment building on New York's **Upper East Side**[2] where plenty of people know her and stop by to see how she is. She just wanted company—and, damn it, I was busy. I continued my business discussion

for another twenty minutes until the second call came.

9   This time my grandmother was genuinely hysterical. "Natalie, WHERE ARE YOU?" she cried. "You said you were coming right over! Please darling."

10   Now I really did hurry, racing out the door and grabbing a cab. But the moment I arrived at her apartment I wanted to run the other way again. She clutched my arm and pulled me inside. Her face was a gray blur of tears and her thin white hair stood up in wild peaks. Her bathrobe had half fallen off; I'd never seen my grandmother's naked body before. The apartment smelled stale. I threw open a window and sat down stiffly on the couch.

11   For the next few minutes I didn't say a word as my grandmother shuffled around the living room, ranting against the world. She complained about my uncle, who had deserted her earlier in the day (he had to go to work). She railed against my mother—her daughter—who was vacationing in Australia. She talked madly about how they were trying to steal her money, how they'd taken away her keys, how they never spent more than ten minutes at a time with her—although I knew only too well that both her children structured their days and nights around her needs.

12   As she sputtered on, I felt more and more helpless and resentful. Finally, my rage overwhelmed my judgment. I stood up and started yelling at her. I told her that nobody and nothing could help her. "The only person who could help you is you!" I said in righteous fury. "Do you understand me? You've got to stop being so damned dependent on everybody!"

13   At which point she let out a piercing shriek of agony and hurled herself on her bed. The only thing I'd accomplished with my idiotic lecture was to heighten both her hysteria and my sense of impotence.

14   My grandmother is 80, but she seems much older. Although she suffers from a host of physical ailments—mild diabetes, glaucoma, asthma, arthritis—her real problems are neurological and psychological. She may have Alzheimer's, she may have been stricken by a series of small, silent strokes. Her doctor isn't sure, and he says that, frankly, the precise diagnosis doesn't matter: her condition is irreversible. What is clear is that she hates being old, she can't stand being left alone for even minutes at a time, and she'll do anything to surround herself with people.

15   These days, much of the family conversation centers on her. What are we going to do about Grandma? Put her in a **nursing home**[3]? (Too awful.) Hire a live-in companion? (Too expensive.) Put her on some new psychotherapeutic medication? (Nothing seems to work.) Not only does my grandmother demand companionship during the day; she also needs somebody around every night. So another question my family grapples with is: whose turn is it to sleep over on Grandmother's sofa bed?

16   By far the most debilitating consequence of the ordeal is the guilt. Because we can't seem to make my grandmother happy, we feel frustrated. That frustration leads us to either explode in anger or to drop out of sight—immature reactions that come prepackaged with

shame. No matter how much she does, my mother worries she's not doing enough. At the same time, she bitterly resents her mother's nonstop demands. The result is that my mother visits and calls my grandmother constantly, but then ends up lashing out in senseless indignation. My uncle usually represses his emotions, but he's starting to gain weight and to look his 56 years.

17 I managed to combine the worst of all worlds. I neglect to call my grandmother for weeks at a stretch. When I do visit, I lapse into the role of **boot-camp**[4] sergeant. As a fitness fanatic, I tell her it's never too late to take up exercise. I turn away from her tears. My mother accuses me of being heartless; she's right.

18 My grandmother is the first person I have watched grow old. I used to adore her: she still keeps loving poems and letters I wrote to her. She was always a vivid, energetic woman, selling bonds for Israel, working long hours in charity **thrift shops**[5]. She told stories about her past with the narrative panache of **Isaac Bashevis Singer**[6]. Wherever she went, she made flocks of friends—a trait that I, a lonely and sullen girl, particularly admired.

19 But then hard times began to pile up around her like layers of choking silt. Although she'd stoutly nursed three husbands through terminal illnesses, she became increasingly depressed when her siblings—all older than she—started to die. After she lost her last remaining sister, in 1982, my grandmother just about lost her mind. She still had many friends, but she clamored for ever more attention from her children and grandchildren. She became an emotional hair-trigger; she'd have temper tantrums at parties, **seders**[7], my sister's wedding.

20 As my grandmother has worsened, so too has my response to her. My mother implores me to be decent and stay in touch, and I launch into all the reasons why I don't. But my excuses sound shallow and glib, even to myself. The truth is that my grandmother terrifies me.

21 I have in my mind a pastel confection of the perfect old woman. She is wise and dignified, at peace with herself and quietly proud of the life she has forged. She doesn't waste time seeking approval or cursing the galaxy. Instead, she works at her craft. She is **Georgia O'Keeffe**[8] painting, **Louise Nevelson**[9] sculpturing, **Marianne Moore**[10] writing. Or she is a less celebrated woman, who reads, listens to **Bach**[11], and threads together the scattered days into a private whole.

22 Of course, there are many things my fantasy doyenne is not. She's not strapped for money. Her joints don't ache, her breath doesn't rattle. She isn't losing her memory, her reason, her eyesight. Above all, she is not the old woman I know best.

23 I love my grandmother. She still has her good hours, when her mind is quick and clear. Inevitably, though, her mad despair bursts to the surface again. She discovers a new reason to weep, blame, and backstab, and I discover a new excuse for staying away.

24 I want to age magnificently, as O'Keeffe and Moore did. I want to be better in half a century than I am at 31, but I doubt that I will. When I look at my grandmother, fragile, frightened, unhappy, wanting to die but clinging desperately to life, I see myself—and I cannot stand the sight.

Notes

① **Natalie Angier** (born February 16, 1958 in Bronx, New York City) is an American nonfiction writer and a science journalist for *The New York Times*.

② **Upper East Side** Sometimes called "New York's Gold Coast," the Upper East Side (from 57th Street to 96th Street, and from East End Avenue to Fifth Avenue) is a wealth of artistic treasures, from those found in the Metropolitan Museum of Art to the Solomon R. Guggenheim Museum to the Frick Collection. (美国)纽约市曼哈顿区的上东部,约在第57街和第96街之间,这里包括许多时髦商店和住宅区

③ **nursing home** old people's home, a place where people who are old and ill can live and be looked after, 疗养院

④ **boot-camp** a training camp for people who have just joined the United States Army, Navy, or Marine Corps, 〈美口〉海军训练新兵之营地

⑤ **charity thrift shops** shops that sell used goods, especially clothes, often in order to earn money for a charity, 〈美〉(为慈善目的而开设、主要出售衣服的)廉价旧货店

⑥ **Isaac Bashevis Singer (1904—1991)** a polish-born American Yiddish writer, winner of the 1978 Nobel Prize for Literature. 辛格,出生于波兰的美国犹太小说家,曾用意第绪语写作,作品有长篇小说《卢布林的魔术师》《奴隶》和短篇小说《傻瓜吉姆佩尔和其他故事》等,获1978年诺贝尔文学奖。

⑦ **Seder** lavish, ceremonial family dinners commemorating the exodus of the Jews from Egypt, celebrated by Jewish people on the first two nights of Passover. (犹太教)逾越节家宴(于犹太教历尼散月之15日和16日举行)

⑧ **Georgia O'Keeffe (1887—1986)** American abstract painter, famous for the purity and lucidity of her still-life compositions. O'Keeffe is best known for her large paintings of desert flowers, sun-bleached animal skulls, and New Mexico landscapes. 奥基夫,美国现代派女画家,以描绘大自然,以及大朵花卉和兽骨等的半抽象画闻名,曾作大量描绘新墨西哥州沙漠的画,作品有《白谷仓,一号》等。

⑨ **Louise Nevelson (1899—1988)** Russian-born American sculptor, best known for her abstract vertical wood sculptures. 路易丝·内维尔森,美国女雕刻家、画家和版画家,以大型单色的抽象雕刻和环境雕刻闻名,代表作品有《墙》等。

⑩ **Marianne Moore (1887—1972)** American poet. Moore's first collection of verse was *Poems* (1921). This book was followed by *Observations* (1924), *Selected Poems of Marianne Moore* (1935), and many others. 穆尔,美国女诗人,作品以对客观事物的观察与表达精辟入微著称,主要作品有《诗集》、诗集《观察》等,后者曾获日晷奖。

⑪ **Johann Sebastian Bach (1685—1750)** German composer and organist of the baroque period. 巴赫,德国作曲家,管风琴家,出身于爱森纳赫的音乐世家,一生作品丰富,多用复调音乐写成,把巴罗克音乐风格推向顶峰,对西方音乐发展有深远影响。

Unit Five

Vocabulary

1. mouthpiece ['maʊθpiːs] *n.* the part, such as of a musical instrument or telephone, that is put into or near the mouth, 话筒
2. heave [hiːv] *v.* to rise and fall regularly, 有规律地起伏, 喘息; (of a person) to give out a deep sound, especially a sad sound, (人)发出(尤指叹息声)
3. gasp [gɑːsp] *vi.* to breathe quickly, especially with difficulty, making a noise in the throat, 急促地呼吸, 发出喘粗气的声音
4. mutter ['mʌtə] *v.* to speak in a low voice, especially out of annoyance or to avoid being heard, 咕哝, 嘀咕
5. hysterical [hɪ'sterɪk(ə)l] *adj.* unable to control behavior or emotions because of fear, excitement, or distress, 歇斯底里的
6. clutch [klʌtʃ] *v.* to suddenly take hold of someone or something because of fear, danger, or pain, 抓住
7. bathrobe ['bɑːθrəʊb] *n.* a long loose piece of clothing shaped like a coat worn before or after a bath or shower, 浴衣
8. stale [steɪl] *adj.* not fresh or pleasant, 不新鲜的, 污浊的
9. shuffle ['ʃʌf(ə)l] *vi.* to walk very slowly and noisily, without lifting the feet off the ground, 拖着脚走
10. rant [rænt] *v.* to talk or complain in a loud and angry manner, 激昂地说
11. sputter ['spʌtə] *v.* to talk quickly in short confused phrases, especially out of anger or shock, 气急败坏地说, 语无伦次地说
12. righteous ['raɪtʃəs] *adj.* (of feelings) morally blameless; having just cause, (情感)道义上无可指责的, 正当的
13. fury ['fjʊərɪ] *n.* extreme, often uncontrolled anger, 狂怒
14. piercing ['pɪəsɪŋ] *adj.* (of sound) very sharp and clear, especially in an unpleasant way, (声音)刺耳的, 尖声的
15. shriek [ʃriːk] *n.* a loud high-pitched sound made out of fright, anger, or excitement, 尖叫, 尖声
16. agony ['ægənɪ] *n.* extreme pain or suffering of mind or body, (身心的)极大痛苦
17. hysteria [hɪ'stɪərɪə] *n.* a condition of uncontrollable nervous excitement or anger, 歇斯底里, 癔病
18. impotence ['ɪmpətəns] *n.* the quality of lacking strength or power, of being weak or feeble, 无力, 虚弱, 无效
19. diabetes [ˌdaɪə'biːtiːz] *n.* a disease in which there is too much sugar in the blood, [医] 糖尿病
20. glaucoma [glɔː'kəʊmə] *n.* an eye disease in which increased pressure inside the eye gradually causes loss of sight, 绿内障, 青光眼
21. asthma ['æsmə] *n.* a medical condition that causes difficulties in breathing, [医]哮喘

22. arthritis [ɑːˈθraɪtɪs] *n.* a disease that causes body joints to become swollen and very painful, 关节炎
23. Alzheimer's [ˈɔːltshaɪmərz] *n.* a disease marked by progressive loss of mental capacity resulting from degeneration of brain cells, [医] 痴呆, 智力衰退
24. irreversible [ɪrɪˈvɜːsɪb(ə)l] *adj.* that which cannot be brought back to a former state, 不可更改的, 不可挽回(撤回)的
25. live-in [ˈlɪvɪn] *adj.* someone who sleeps and eats in a house where he or she is employed; someone who lives with someone else, 住在雇主家的; 食住在一起的
26. therapeutic [ˌθerəˈpjuːtɪk] *adj.* of or for the treating or curing of disease, 治疗(学)的, 疗法的, 起治疗作用的
27. debilitate [dɪˈbɪlɪteɪt] *vt.* to make weak, especially through heat, illness, or hunger, 使虚弱, 使衰弱
28. ordeal [ɔːˈdiːəl] *n.* a difficult or painful experience, 严峻的考验; 苦难的经历
29. senseless [ˈsenslɪs] *adj.* happening or done for no good reason or for no purpose, 毫无意义的, 无目的的, 愚蠢的
30. indignation [ɪndɪgˈneɪʃ(ə)n] *n.* feelings of surprised anger (because of something wrong or unjust), (因错事或不公正事而感到的)愤怒, 愤慨, 义愤
31. repress [rɪˈpres] *vt.* to control, hold back, or prevent natural expression, such as of a feeling, desire, or action, 抑止; 控制
32. panache [pəˈnæʃ] *n.* a stylish and seemingly effortless manner of doing things that causes admiration, flair, 潇洒; 麻利; 神奇十足
33. sullen [ˈsʌlən] *adj.* silently showing dislike or bad temper, 闷闷不乐的, 默默地发着脾气的; 样子很不高兴的
34. silt [sɪlt] *n.* sand, mud, soil that is carried in water and then settles in such places as at a bend in a river or an entrance to a port, 淤泥, 泥沙
35. stoutly [ˈstaʊtli] *adv.* bravely, determinedly, resolutely, 刚强地, 坚决地
36. sibling [ˈsɪblɪŋ] *n.* a brother or sister, 兄弟或姐妹
37. clamor [ˈklæmə] *vi.* to express (a demand) continuously, loudly, and strongly, 大声疾呼, 强烈要求
38. hair-trigger [heəˈtrɪgə] *n.* very quickly and easily angered by the slightest provocation or stimulation, 一触即发的状态
39. tantrum [ˈtæntrəm] *n.* a sudden short burst of intense and unreasonable anger, 发脾气, 发怒
40. implore [ɪmˈplɔː] *vt.* to ask for in a begging manner, 祈求, 恳求, 哀求
41. shallow [ˈʃæləʊ] *adj.* lacking deep or serious thinking, superficial, 肤浅的, 浅薄的
42. glib [glɪb] *adj.* spoken too easily, without thought and often without sincerity, 流利而不真实的, 油嘴滑舌的
43. pastel [ˈpæst(ə)l] *adj.* drawn in pastels, 彩色蜡笔的; soft and light in color, 柔和的
44. confection [kənˈfekʃ(ə)n] *n.* something, especially a piece of clothing or a building, that is of delicate design, complicated, or highly decorated, 精制工艺品

Unit Five

45. dignified [ˈdɪgnɪfaɪd] *adj.* behaving in a calm and serious way, even in a difficult situation, such as to produce respect, 有威严的,有品格的
46. celebrated [ˈselɪbreɪtɪd] *adj.* well-known, famous, 著名的
47. doyenne [dɔɪˈen] *n.* the oldest, most respected, or most experienced woman in a group, 女性老前辈
48. strap [stræp] *vt.* to fasten into place with one or more long narrow bands, e.g., of leather, plastic, or metal, 用带缚住,用带捆扎
49. rattle [ˈræt(ə)l] *vi.* to make a rapid succession of short sharp noises,(因呼吸困难)发呼噜声
50. backstab [ˈbækˌstæb] *v.* to undercut or speak evil of someone behind his or her back, especiallyl to gain an advantage, 以卑鄙的手段陷害
51. fragile [ˈfrædʒaɪl] *adj.* not in a good condition of health or spirits, weak, delicate, 虚弱的,精神不振的,有气无力的

Useful Expressions

1. **come over:** to arrive; to make a short informal visit; to change sides
    (1) After we had discussed our differences, he decided to come over to our point of view.
    (2) When did you first come over to China?
    (3) Come over and see us when you come back to Beijing.
2. **hang up:** to finish a telephone conversation by putting the receiver back
    (1) It's a bad line; hang up and I'll call you back.
    (2) Don't hang up on me—I need to talk with you.
    (3) I was so angry that I hung up on him.
3. **let out:** to express loudly and violently
    (1) Hearing the good news, the boy let out a cry of joy.
    (2) Henry let out a long and slow breath and stared up at the brilliant blue sky.
    (3) He let out a deep breath to show his disappointment.
4. **center on:** have as a main subject or area of concern
    (1) His interests are centered on seeking fame and money.
    (2) The dispute centers on how to pay for the overtime work.
    (3) The topic centers on the crisis in these two countries.
5. **grapple with:** to work hard to deal with something difficult
    (1) Don't interrupt me; I'm grappling with accounts.
    (2) The newly elected prime minister has a grave economic crisis to grapple with.
    (3) The government has to grapple with the problem of escalating crime rates.
6. **lash out (at):** to make a sudden violent attacking speech or movement
    (1) In his speech the judge lashes out against the drug dealers.
    (2) It seemed that he was going to lash out at her, bue he controlled himself.

(3) Some Arabs have lashed out at the terrorist groups for the bomb blast which killed many innocent people.

7. **at a stretch**: without stopping

    (1) She has been working for hours at a stretch.

    (2) There's no way I could work for ten hours at a stretch.

    (3) A lion can lie in the same spot without moving for twelve hours at a stretch.

8. **lapse into**: to pass gradually into a less active or less desirable state

    (1) No one could think of anything more to say, and the meeting lapsed into silence.

    (2) After a year of fame the singer lapsed back into obscurity.

    (3) He has lapsed once again into his old smoking habits.

9. **accuse of:** to charge with doing wrong or breaking the law

    (1) No one in this department has ever accused the governor of taking advantage of his position; he is hard-working and considerate.

    (2) Critics accused the writer of a lack of originality.

    (3) I was accused of stealing money from her; but in fact it was the other way round.

10. **pile up:** to put (one thing) on top of another, to form a pile; to move in a mass or in masses

    (1) The work has been piling up for days. I'm beginning to wonder if it will ever stop!

    (2) People are dying one after another, and their dead bodies are piling up.

    (3) The clouds are piling up. It's going to rain.

11. **launch into:** to suddenly start doing something

    (1) He tried his best to keep her from launching into topics that might betray the fact that he didn't know her.

    (2) I sat down at the piano and launched into Bach's "Toccata in C Major."

    (3) The opposition launched into a violent attack on the government.

12. **cling to:** to hold tightly, refuse to go or let go, stick firmly

    (1) He clung to the hope that he would succeed.

    (2) They clung to each other for support.

    (3) He has been watching for every piece of mail as he clings to a hope that one day his missing brother will contact him.

13. **end up:** to be (unexpectedly) in a particular situation, state, or place after a series of events

    (1) I ended up having to pay for everyone's dinner.

    (2) After swimming at night, we all ended up with colds.

    (3) Somewhat to her surprise she ended up designing the whole car and putting it into production.

14. **be strapped for:** to be in need of

    (1) He is always strapped for cash the week before pay day; he cannot make his money last from one pay day to the next.

    (2) At the end of the semester, everyone is strapped for time.

    (3) When my car broke down, I was strapped for transportation.

Unit Five

Understanding the Text

1. In the eyes of Natalie Angier, what was her aging grandma like? Is it a flattering description?
2. What emotions did her grandmother excite in her?
3. How did the needs and demands of her grandmother frustrate her mother and her uncle?
4. How do you imagine the aging of Georgia O'Keeffe and Marianne Moore?
5. Do you have the same fear as Natalie?
6. Describe Angier's fantasy of "the perfect old woman." How does Angier's grandmother differ from this ideal?
7. Angier explores two related causal chains: the effect of the grandmother's decline on the family and the reasons for the grandmother's decline. Which causal chain does Angier explore first? Why?
8. Angier's causal analysis includes a strong narrative component. As such, it focuses on a number of conflicts. What conflicts do you detect in this text?
9. In the narrative parts of her essay, Angier uses dialogue fairly often, mixing actual dialogues (Paragraphs 2, 3, 5, 6, 7, 9, and 12) and dialogue paraphrasing (Paragraph 4). Why might she have chosen first-hand dialogue in some places and second-hand paraphrasing in others? What effect does each of these narrative techniques have on the way the story is told?

Exercises

A. Fill in the blanks with the appropriate words from the text.

1. I _____ and told my colleague that I'd have to leave in a few minutes. But I didn't believe there was any _____ . When I _____ the door and _____ a cab and hurried to my grandmother's apartment, it was just as I expected.
2. I kept silent as my grandmother _____ the living room, _____ the world with a gray blur of tears on her face and her thin white hair _____ in wild peaks.
3. As her grandmother _____ , Natalie felt so _____ that her rage _____ her judgment. Finally she stood up and yelled at her grandmother. The result was that her grandmother _____ a piercing _____ of agony and _____ herself on her bed.
4. Although her grandmother suffers from _____ physical ailments—mild diabetes, asthma, arthritis—the author believes her real problems lie in that she _____ being old; she can't _____ being left alone for even minutes _____ . To make her grandmother happy, the family is now discussing whether to put her in a _____ or hire a _____ companion.

5. They feel guilty for not being able to please grandmother, which leads them to either _____ in anger or to drop _____. The author neglects to call her for weeks _____. When she pays a visit, she _____ the role of boot-camp sergeant... her mother_____ her _____ being heartless.

B. **Choose from the words given below to complete the following sentences, changing the word form where necessary.**

stale	indignation	stand	dignified
heighten	ordeal	fragile	sullen
senseless	irreversible	agony	implore
backstab	piercing	repress	celebrated

1. I expressed my _____ at being unfairly frozen out.
2. The criminal _____ the judge for mercy.
3. Suzhou is _____ for its beautiful gardens.
4. The room smells of _____ cigar smoke. Open a window, please.
5. He can't _____ being kept waiting.
6. The campaign is intended to _____ public awareness of the disease.
7. The _____ girl refused to answer her sister's questions.
8. Because her bones were so _____, they broke easily under the slightest pressure.
9. Jack burst in, making no effort to _____ his fury.
10. Her father could suffer _____ brain damage if he is not treated within seven days.

C. **Fill in the blanks with the phrases given below, changing the form where necessary.**

come over	pile up	lash out	lapse into
grapple with	end up	cling to	hang up
let out	launch into	accuse of	center on

1. He _____ the hope that his wife would be cured.
2. They were walking along the beach when she suddenly _____ in anger at her boyfriend.
3. After leaving college, David _____ a business career.
4. She _____ that night to see how I was doing.
5. The injured dog _____ sharp cries.
6. As soon as he had _____, he went over to the workmen and told them that if a policeman ordered them to go away, they were not to take him seriously.
7. She _____ stealing twenty-five pounds from her boss.
8. He _____ the problem for a long time but failed to work out a solution.
9. If you don't know what you want, you might _____ getting something you don't want.
10. Burning garbage might be a method to reduce the amount of garbage _____ on the earth.

Unit Five

D. Fill in the blanks with the expressions given below, changing the form where necessary.

by far	turn away from	gain weight
hair-trigger	at peace with	be stricken by
out of sight	rant against	take up exercise
burst to the surface	stay in touch	work at one's craft
at a stretch	be strapped for	be informed of
come prepackaged with	lose one's mind	

1. To walk ten miles _____ was not an easy job.
2. We all need to _____ with friends and family no matter where we are or what we are doing.
3. As a successful actress, she has been spending years learning and _____.
4. She _____ her boyfriend and began to cry.
5. This is _____ the largest bridge in the world.
6. Leave any valuables _____.
7. Most patients' first reaction to their terminal illness _____ is to deny the reality of the situation.
8. Jack really _____ after his wife left him.
9. I'm _____ these days. I think I'd better take some diet pills.
10. He has been really _____ cash because he lost his job two weeks ago.

E. Read the following text and choose the best word for each blank from the choices given.

America is a youth, health and career obsessed society.

Looking around America, you'll notice that most faces (1) _____ billboards, magazines, TV, and advertisements are (2) _____ of young, pretty people. In a culture that equates youth (3) _____ beauty, a majority of Americans are (4) _____ at war with aging. Before the advent of new technologies, people used to jump through hoops to shave a couple years (5) _____ their looks. But now, laser surgery is a relatively painless (6) _____ to facelifts and skin tucks(拉皮). And let us not forget all the fancy anti-aging cosmetic products and skin treatments in department stores and beauty (7) _____. Furthermore, we have also developed holistic approaches (8) _____ fighting aging: yoga, herbs, acupuncture.

It seems like people will do (9) _____ anything to stay young. But the crazy thing is that you can't stay young (10) _____. That's impossible. What you can do is feel youthful. And that requires much (11) _____ cosmetic changes. In order to feel young, you must exercise your mind, (12) _____ with the world, and maintain an active lifestyle. In (13) _____ words, instead of spending $5000 on wrinkle-removing laser surgery, why not go (14) _____ an adventurous journey to an unfamiliar part of the world? Instead of spending $50 on a bottle of anti-aging lotion, why not buy a mountain bike?

We should always remember the fountain of youth (15) _____ in our heart, mind, and spirit.

1. A. in   B. on   C. from   D. of
2. A. those   B. that   C. the one   D. ones

3. A. with	B. as	C. to	D. for
4. A. successively	B. continuously	C. constantly	D. frequently
5. A. of	B. off	C. from	D. out of
6. A. change	B. choice	C. option	D. alternative
7. A. houses	B. saloons	C. salons	D. offices
8. A. to	B. for	C. out	D. against
9. A. hardly	B. almost	C. seldom	D. closely
10. A. ever	B. moreover	C. lifelong	D. forever
11. A. more than	B. less than	C. rather than	D. more
12. A. keep up	B. match up	C. come up	D. correspond
13. A. another	B. else	C. other	D. selective
14. A. for	B. to	C. on	D. out
15. A. lies	B. results	C. takes	D. sets

F. Translate the following sentences into English, using the phrases and expressions given in parentheses.

1. 她很生儿子的气，就挂断了他的电话。(hang up)
2. 在得知自己被开除的消息时，他发出了愤怒的吼声。(let out)
3. 公众的注意力集中在下周的总统选举上。(center on)
4. 他花了一个小时才解出了那道题。(grapple with)
5. 她似乎就要斥责他了，但马上又控制住了自己。(lash out)
6. 他们不得不连续站立好几个小时。(at a stretch)
7. 服药后，她进入了深睡状态。(lapse into)
8. 她仍然抱着这样的信念：她的丈夫还活着，有一天会回家来的。(cling to)
9. 我们没能赶上这一场现场表演，最终还是在电视屏幕上欣赏它。(end up)
10. 经理桌上堆满了要看的资料，她知道今晚又得开夜车了。(pile up)

Text B

Stay Young
Marya Mannes[①]

1. Like all people in the middle span, I am aware of death and saddened by its advance forces of disintegration. I do not like the signs in flesh and muscle and bone of slow decline, even if they are yet unaccompanied by pain. To one in love with physical beauty, its inevitable blurring by years is a source of melancholy.

2 Yet I feel sure that while the flesh may retreat before age, the man or woman can advance if he goes towards death rather than away from it, if he understands the excitement implicit in this progression from the part to the whole. For that is, really, what it should be: a steady ascent from personal involvement—the paths and rocks and valleys and rises of the foothills—to the ultimate height where they fuse into one grand and complex pattern, remote and yet rewarding. It is like coming into clearer air. And if that air becomes in course too rare to breathe, the final breath is one of total purity.

3 It is because of these convictions that I protest against the American tyranny of youth. There is beauty and freshness in youth (if there is less and less innocence), but it is an accident of time and therefore ephemeral. There is no "trick" in being young: it happens to you. But the process of maturing is an art to be learned, an effort to be sustained. By the age of fifty you have made yourself what you are, and if it is good, it is better than your youth. If it is bad, it is not because you are older but because you have not grown.

4 Yet all this is obscured, daily, hourly, by the selling barrage of youth, perhaps the greatest campaign for the **arrested development**[2] of the human being ever waged anywhere. Look young, be young, stay young, they call from every page and on every air wave. You must be young to be loved. And with this mandate, this threat, this pressure, millions of goods are sold and millions of hours are spent in pursuit of a youth which no longer exists and which cannot be recaptured.

5 The result of this effort is, in women, obscene; in men, pathetic. For the American woman of middle age thinks of youth only in terms of appearance and the American man of middle age thinks of youth only in terms of virility.

6 If obscene seems a strong word to use for old women who try to look young, I will be more explicit. It is quite true and quite proper that better eating habits, better care, and less drudgery have made American women look ten years younger than their mothers did at the same age. One of the pleasing phenomena of our life is the naturally young and pretty grandmother, almost as lithe and active as her daughter. But I am talking of the still older woman, past her middle fifties, often alone, often idle, who has the means to spend the greater part of her leisure in beauty salons and shops and weight-reducing parlors, resisting age with desperate intensity. They do not know it, but the fact of this resistance nullifies the effects of the effort. The streets of American cities are full of these thin, massaged, made-up, corseted, tinted, overdressed women with faces that are repellent masks of frustration: hard, empty, avid. Although their ankles are slender and their feet perched on backless high-heeled slippers, they fool no one, and certainly no man. They are old legs and old feet. Although their flesh is clear and fairly firm in the visible areas, it is kneaded flesh, and fools no one. The hips are small indeed, but the girdle only emphasizes their stiff aridity. And the uplift bra, the **platinum hair**[3], the tight dress? Whom do they fool? The woman herself, alone. And the obscenity in all this is that she uses the outward techniques of sexual allure to maintain her youth when she is no longer wanted by men. And she does it because she has

been told to do it by the advertising media. She has been sold a bill of goods.

7   Let me hastily say at this point that it is the solemn duty of all women to look as well as they can and to maintain through life the grooming that makes them pleasing to others. Towards this end, the advertisers have performed a signal service to Americans. But they have over-reached themselves, and us. Instead of saying "Be Yourself," they say "Be Young." Instead of saying "Relax," they say "Compete!" In doing this, they deprive the maturing woman of a great joy, an astounding relief: the end, not of sex, heaven knows, but of sexual competition. By the time a woman is fifty she is either wanted as a woman of fifty or not really wanted at all. She does not have to fool her husband or her lover, and she knows that competition with women far younger than she is not only degrading but futile.

8   It is also an axiom that the more time a woman spends on herself, the less she has for others and the less desirable she is to others. If this goes for young women—and I believe it does—it goes doubly for older women, who have—if they knew it—more to give.

9   When I go to Europe and see the old people in villages in France or Italy, for instance, I am struck at once by the age of all women who are no longer young, pitying their premature withering, and at the same time startled by the occasional beauty of their old faces. Lined and grooved and puckered as they may be, their hair grizzled or lank, there is something in their eyes and in their bones that gives age austerity and makes their glossy contemporaries at a bridge table here seem parodies of women. They show that they have lived and they have not yet found the means to hide it.

10 I remember also that as a child and a young girl I never thought of my mother in terms of age. Whatever it was at any time, she looked it; and nobody then told her to lose weight or do something about her hair because she was far too interesting a human being to need such "ameliorations." It would, indeed, have been an impertinence. My mother had no illusions of beauty: she was too concerned with music and her husband and her children to be concerned, in detail, with herself. I don't doubt that, given today's aids, she could have looked younger and smarter than she did. But she would have lost something. The time and effort spent in improving her looks would have been taken from music and from love. With her unruly eyebrows plucked to a thin line, her face made-up, her plump, small body moulded into girdles, an important part of her would have vanished: her identity.

11 It is this that the older women of America are losing. At club gatherings, at hotels, at resorts, they look identical. What lives they have led have been erased from their faces along with the more obvious marks of age. They have smoothed and hardened into a mould. Their lotions have done well.

12 It could be said that if they maintain the illusion of youth to themselves only, no harm is done and some good. But I wonder if all self-deceptions do not harm, and if their price is not loss of self.

13 I wonder too whether one of the reasons for wild, intemperate, destructive youth might not be this same hard finish, this self-absorption, of the women to whom they might

otherwise turn. I cannot imagine going for counsel and comfort to a mother or aunt or grandmother tightly buttressed by latex and heavily masked by make-up. Where is the soft wide lap, the old kind hands, the tender face of age?

14. None of us with any pride in person and any sense of aesthetics can allow ourselves to crumble into decay without trying to slow the process or at least veil its inroads. But that is not the major battle. The fight is not for what is gone but for what is coming; and for this the fortification of the spirit is paramount, the preservation of the flesh a trivial second.

15. Let the queen bee keep her royal jelly. Or so I keep telling myself.

Notes

① **Marya Mannes** (1904—1990) Marya Mannes was an American novelist, poet, and essayist, who worked as a staff writer for *Reporter* magazine. Her published books include *The New York I Know* (1961), *But Will It Sell* (1964), *Subverse* (poems, 1964), and *Out of My Time* (1971).
② **arrested development** an interruption of the movement toward maturity, 发育不良
③ **platinum hair** hair dyed a silvery white, 银灰色的头发

Exercises

A. Understanding the text.

1. In what terms do American women think of youth? In what contrasting terms do American men think of youth?
2. What does the author think advertisers should be saying to women? What are they actually saying instead?
3. In what countries is the author often struck by the natural beauty of older women who do not try to hide their age?

B. Choose the best answer to each of the following questions.

1. According to the author, what must a man or woman do to advance with old age?
    A. Improve one's eating habits, have better care, and avoid drudgery.
    B. Spend more time and money to preserve youth.
    C. Understand it is a natural process to become old and accept it.
    D. All of the above.
2. From the passage, we can conclude that ____.
    A. the author is an optimistic person
    B. the author welcomes aging
    C. the older a person is, the wiser he or she becomes
    D. the older a woman is, the better she knows how to make herself up

3. What does the author imply when she says, "In doing this, they deprive the maturing woman of a great joy, an astounding relief: the end, not of sex, heaven knows, but of sexual competition" (Paragraph 7)?

   A. By selling maturing women products to stay young, advertisers promote the myth that one must be young to be loved and accepted.

   B. In using advertised beauty aids, maturing women show that they do not need to compete with other women any more.

   C. Using beauty products helps maturing women to be very confident about their glamour.

   D. Advertisers create a sense of competition between maturing women and young women.

4. What price do women pay for their attempts at deceiving themselves and the world about how old they are?

   A. They lose their identity and sense of self-worth.

   B. They lose their husband and children.

   C. They lose the trust of others.

   D. They forget how old they are.

5. What does the word "ameliorations" (Paragraph 10) mean?

   A. Decoration.

   B. Modification.

   C. Make-up.

   D. Improvement.

6. From Paragraph 14, we can learn that the major battle for a woman is _____.

   A. to strengthen her sense of aesthetics

   B. to preserve her appearance

   C. to slow the process of aging

   D. to look forward rather than backward

On-the-job Writing: Proposals

The general purpose of any proposal is to persuade the reader to do something, whether it is (1) to persuade a potential customer to purchase your products and services or (2) to persuade your management to fund a project you would like to launch. You would write a sales proposal to accomplish the first objective; you would write an internal proposal to accomplish the second. An internal proposal is normally prepared as a memo, by either an employee or a department, and sent to a higher-ranking person in the same organization.

Short or medium- length proposals basically consist of an introduction, a body, and a conclusion. The *introduction* should summarize the problem you are proposing to solve and your solution to it; it may also indicate the benefits that your reader will receive from your solution and the total cost of the solution. The *body* should explain in complete detail exactly (1) how the job will be done, (2) what methods will be used to do it (and, if applicable, the specific materials to be used and any other pertinent information, (3) when work will begin, (4) when the job will be completed, and (5) the detailed cost breakdown for the entire job. The *conclusion* should emphasize the benefits that the reader will realize from your solution to the problem and should urge the reader to action. Your conclusion should have an encouraging, confident, and reasonably assertive tone.

Give your evidence in descending order of importance: that is, begin with the most important evidence and end with the least important. Anticipate and answer any objections your reader may have to your approach to the problem and your solution to it. Consider any alternative solutions that might be offered and show how yours is superior to them.

Sample Proposal

ACME Inc.
INTEROFFICE MEMO

To: Joan Marlow, Director, Human Resources Division
From: Leslie Galusha, Chief, Employee Benefits Department
Date: June 12, 2018
Subject: Employee Fitness and Health-Care Costs

Health-care and worker-compensation insurance costs at Acme, Inc. have risen 200 percent over the last few years. In 2012, costs were $600 per employee per year; in 2017, they reached $1,200 per employee per year. This doubling of costs mirrors a national trend, with health-care costs anticipated to continue to rise at the same rate for the next 10 years. The U.S. Department of Health and Human Services recently estimated that health-care costs in the United States will triple by the year 2020. Controlling these escalating expenses will be essential. They are eating into Acme's profit margin because the company currently pays 80 percent of the costs for employee coverage.

Researchers have found that people who do not participate in a regular and vigorous exercise program incur double the health-care costs and are hospitalized 30 percent more days than people who exercise regularly. Healthy employees bring direct financial benefits to companies in the form of lower employee insurance costs, lower absenteeism rates, and reduced turnover. Regular physical exercise promotes fit, healthy people by reducing the risk of coronary heart disease, diabetes, osteoporosis, hypertension, and stress-related problems. I propose that to promote regular, vigorous physical exercise for our employees, Acme implement a health-care program that focuses on employee fitness.

SOLUTION

I propose that we choose from one of two possible options: build in-house fitness centers at our warehouse facilities or offer employees several options for membership at a national fitness club.

In-house Fitness Center

Building in-house fitness centers would require that Acme modify existing space in its warehouses and designate an area outside for walking and running. To accommodate the weight lifting and cardiovascular equipment and an aerobics area would require a minimum of 4,000 square feet. Lockers and shower stalls would also have to be built adjacent to the men's and women's bathrooms.

The costs to equip each facility are as follows:

1 Challenger 3.0 Treadmill	$4,395
3 Ross Futura exercise bicycles $750 each	$2,250
1 CalGym S-370 inner thigh machine	$1,750
1 CalGym S-260 lat pull-down machine	$1,750
1 CalGym S-360 leg-extension, combo-curl	$1,650
1 CalGym S-390 arm-curl machine	$1,950
1 CalGym S-410 side-lat machine	$1,850
1 CalGym S-430 pullover machine	$1,950
1 CalGym S-440 abdominal machine	$2,000
1 CalGym S-460 back machine	$2,000
1 CalGym S-290 chest press	$1,600
1 CalGym S-310 pectoral developer	$1,700
10 5710321 3-wide lockers $81 each	$810
4 5714000 benches and pedestals $81 each	$324
Carpeting for workout area	$3,000
3 showers each, men's/women's locker room	$10,000
Men's and women's locker-room expansion	$10,000
Remodeling expenses	$350,000
Total per Acme site	$398,979
Grand Total	**$1,994,895**

At headquarters and at the regional offices, our current Employee Assistance Program staff would need to be available several hours each work day to provide instructions for the use of exercise equipment. Aerobics instructors can be hired locally on a monthly basis for classes. The Buildings and Maintenance Department staff would clean and maintain the facilities.

Fitness-Club Membership

Offering a complimentary membership to a national fitness club for all employees can also help reduce company health-care costs. AeroFitness Clubs, Inc., offers the best option for Acme's needs. They operate in over 45 major markets, with over 300 clubs nationwide. Most importantly, AeroFitness clubs are located here in Bartlesville and in all four cities where our regional warehouses are located.

The club offers a full range of membership programs for companies. Acme may choose to pay all or part of employee membership costs. Three membership program options are available with AeroFitness*:

Corporate purchase. Acme buys and owns the membership. With 10 or more memberships, Acme receives a 35% discount.

Acme costs: $400 per employee × 1200 employees–35% discount = $312,000 per year.

Corporate subsidy. Employees purchase memberships at a discount and own them. With 10 or more memberships, employees and the company each pay one-half of annual membership dues and receive a 30% discount off annual dues. The corporation also pays a one-time $50 enrollment fee.

Acme costs: $200 per employee × 1200 employees–30% discount = $168,000 per year. The one-time enrollment fee of $50 per employee adds $60,000 to first-year costs.

Employee purchase. Employees purchase memberships on their own. With five or more memberships, employees receive 25% off regular rates. Club sales representatives conduct an onsite open enrollment meeting. Employees own memberships.

Acme costs: None.

*Assume that all employees will enroll.

CONCLUSION AND RECOMMENDATION

I recommend that Acme, Inc., participate in the corporate membership program at AeroFitness Clubs by subsidizing employee memberships. By subsidizing memberships, Acme shows its commitment to the importance of a fit workforce. Club membership allows employees at all five Acme warehouses to participate in the program. The more employees who participate, the greater the long-term savings in Acme's health-care costs. Building and equipping fitness centers at all five warehouse sites would require an initial investment of nearly $2 million. These facilities would also occupy valuable floor space—on average, 4,000 square feet at each warehouse. Therefore, this option would be very costly.

Enrolling employees in the corporate program at AeroFitness would allow them to attend on a trial basis. Those interested in continuing could then join the club and pay half of the membership cost, i.e. a 30% discount on $400 a year. The other half of the membership would be paid by Acme. If an employee leaves the company, he or she would have the option of purchasing Acme's share of the membership. Employees not wishing to keep their membership could buy the membership back from Acme and sell it to another employee.

Implementing this program will help Acme, Inc. reduce its health-care costs while building stronger employee relations by offering them a desirable benefit. If this proposal is adopted, I have some additional thoughts about publicizing the program to encourage employee participation. I look forward to discussing the details of this proposal with you and answering any questions you may have.

Unit Six

Text A

Pre-reading Activities

1. Do you prefer thin people or fat people? Why?
2. Are there any distinct differences in personality between thin people and fat people?
3. What specific characteristics do you associate with thin people and fat people?
4. What could the following terms refer to? What connotations do they carry?

   narrow fellows   skinny
   the wizened and shriveled the chubbies
   bony

That Lean and Hungry Look[①]
Suzanne Britt[②]

1   Caesar was right. Thin people need watching. I've been watching them for most of my adult life, and I don't like what I see. When these narrow fellows spring at me, I quiver to my toes. Thin people come in all personalities, most of them menacing. You've got your "together" thin person, your mechanical thin person, your condescending thin person, your tsk-tsk thin person, your efficiency-expert thin person. All of them are dangerous.

2   In the first place, thin people aren't fun. They don't know how to goof off, at least in the best, fat sense of the word. They've always got to be adoing. Give them a coffee break, and they'll jog around the block. Supply them with a quiet evening at home, and they'll fix the screen door and lick **S&H green stamps**[③]. They say things like "There aren't enough hours in the day." Fat people never say that. Fat people think the day is too damn long already.

3   Thin people make me tired. They've got speedy little metabolisms that cause them to bustle briskly. They're forever rubbing their bony hands together and eyeing new problems to "tackle." I like to surround myself with sluggish, inert, easygoing fat people, the kind who believe that if you clean it up today, it'll just get dirty again tomorrow.

4   Some people say the business about the jolly fat person is a myth, that all of us chubbies are neurotic, sick, sad people. I disagree. Fat people may not be chortling all day long, but they're a hell of a lot nicer than the wizened and shriveled. Thin people turn surly, mean,

and hard at a young age because they never learn the value of a hot-fudge sundae for easing tension. Thin people don't like gooey soft things because they themselves are neither gooey nor soft. They are crunchy and dull, like carrots. They go straight to the heart of the matter while fat people let things stay all blurry and hazy and vague, the way things actually are. Thin people want to face the truth. Fat people know there is no truth. One of my thin friends is always staring at complex, unsolvable problems and saying, "The key thing is..." Fat people never say that. They know there isn't any such thing as the key thing about anything.

5   Thin people believe in logic. Fat people see all sides. The sides fat people see are rounded blobs, usually gray, always nebulous and truly not worth worrying about. But the thin person persists. "If you consume more calories than you burn," says one of my thin friends, "you will gain weight. It's that simple." Fat people always grin when they hear statements like that. They know better.

6   Fat people realize that life is illogical and unfair. They know very well that God is not in his heaven and all is not right with the world. If God were up there, fat people could have two doughnuts and a big orange drink anytime they wanted it.

7   Thin people have a long list of logical things they are always spouting off to me. They hold up one finger at a time as they reel off these things, so I won't lose track. They speak slowly as if to a young child. The list is long and full of holes. It contains tidbits like "get a grip on yourself," "cigarettes kill," "cholesterol clogs," "fit as a fiddle," "ducks in a row," "organize" and "sound fiscal management." Phrases like that.

8   They think these 2,000-point plans lead to happiness. Fat people know happiness is elusive at best and even if they could get the kind thin people talk about, they wouldn't want it. Wisely, fat people see that such programs are too dull, too hard, too off the mark. They are never better than a whole cheesecake.

9   Fat people know all about the mystery of life. They are the ones acquainted with the night, with luck, with fate, with playing it by ear. One thin person I know once suggested that we arrange all the parts of a jigsaw puzzle into groups according to size, shape, and color. He figured this would cut the time needed to complete the puzzle by at least 50 per cent. I said I wouldn't do it. One, I like to muddle through. Two, what good would it do to finish early? Three, the jigsaw puzzle isn't the important thing. The important thing is the fun of four people (one thin person included) sitting around a card table, working a jigsaw puzzle. My thin friend had no use for my list. Instead of joining us, he went outside and mulched the boxwoods. The three remaining fat people finished the puzzle and made chocolate double-fudged brownies to celebrate.

10 The main problem with thin people is they oppress. Their good intentions, bony torsos, tight ships, neat corners, cerebral machinations and pat solutions loom like dark clouds over the loose, comfortable, spread-out, soft world of the fat. Long after fat people have removed their coats and shoes and put their feet up on the coffee table, thin people are still sitting on the edge of the sofa, looking neat as a pin, discussing rutabagas. Fat people are heavily into

fits of laughter, slapping their thighs, and whooping it up, while thin people are still politely waiting for the punch line.

11 Thin people are downers. They like math and morality and reasoned evaluation of the limitations of human beings. They have their skinny little acts together. They expound, prognose, probe, and prick.

12 Fat people are convivial. They will like you even if you're irregular and have acne. They will come up with a good reason why you never wrote the great American novel. They will cry in your beer with you. They will put your name in the pot. They will let you off the hook. Fat people will gab, giggle, guffaw, gallumph, gyrate, and gossip. They are generous, giving, and gallant. They are gluttonous and goodly and great. What you want when you're down is soft and jiggly, not muscled and stable. Fat people know this. Fat people have plenty of room. Fat people will take you in.

Notes

① **That lean and hungry look** a phrase from the play *Julius Caesar* by William Shakespeare. Caesar remarks, concerning one of the men conspiring against him:

   Let me have men about me that are fat,
   Sleek-headed men and such as sleep o' nights;
   Yond' Cassius has a lean and hungry look;
   He thinks too much: such men are dangerous. (I, ii, 189—92)

Caesar means that Cassius looks dangerously dissatisfied, as if he were starved for power. 出自莎士比亚名剧《恺撒大帝》中恺撒对密谋反对他的Cassius所做的评论。剧中恺撒认为Cassius看起来非常危险，似乎没有得到满足，渴望权力。作者援引此作为题目，用来揶揄瘦人。

② **Suzanne Britt** was born in Winston-Salem, North Carolina, and studied at Salem College and Washington University, where she earned an M. A. in English.

③ **S&H green stamps** S&H (the Sperry and Hutchinson Company) began issuing trading stamps (small pieces of gummed paper to be pasted into a booklet) in 1896 and sold its stamps to retailers for use as customer incentives. The retailers gave the stamps to customers, typically at a rate of one for each ten cents worth of purchases, as a bonus for their patronage. Customers would then paste the stamps in booklets of 1,200 stamps and exchange the booklets for "gifts" at S&H redemption centers. S&H green stamps were regarded as a fixture of mid-twentieth-century American shopping and possibly the first customer-loyalty program. Lots of people, especially baby boomers, remember licking green stamps and pasting them in a *TV Guide*-sized book. 20世纪30年代到70年代在美国盛行的一种为刺激消费，由S&H公司发行的一种绿色票券。顾客购物时，零售商会根据顾客购物金额而返回一定数额的绿色票券。顾客可以根据积攒的一定数目的S&H票券到S&H兑换中心兑换相应的书籍或礼物。

Unit Six

Vocabulary

1. menacing [ˈmenɪsɪŋ] *adj.* portending something unpleasant, threatening, 造成威胁的
2. condescending [kɒndɪˈsendɪŋ] *adj.* behaving as though one considers him or herself better, more intelligent, or more important than other people, having a superior manner, 屈尊的, 高傲的
3. tsk-tsk [tɪsktɪsk] *int.* a sound to show disapproval, (表示不赞成、同情、不耐烦等)啧啧
4. jog [dʒɒg] *v.* to run slowly and steadily, especially for exercise, (使)慢跑
5. metabolism [mɪˈtæbəlɪz(ə)m] *n.* chemical processes in the body that cause food to be broken down and synthesized, 新陈代谢(作用)
6. bustle [ˈbʌs(ə)l] *vi.* to move around quickly, looking very busy, 奔忙
7. briskly [ˈbrɪsklɪ] *adv.* quickly and energetically, 活泼地, 精神勃勃地
8. tackle [ˈtæk(ə)l] *v.* to try to deal with a difficult problem, 应付(难事等), 处理, 解决
9. sluggish [ˈslʌgɪʃ] *adj.* moving or reacting more slowly than normal, 不好动的, 懒怠的
10. inert [ɪˈnɜːt] *adj.* not moving or not able to move, 呆滞的, 迟缓的; 无生气的
11. jolly [ˈdʒɒlɪ] *adj.* happy and cheerful, jovial, 欢乐的, 高兴的, 快活的
12. chubby [ˈtʃʌbɪ] *adj.* (especially of children) fat in a pleasant and attractive way, 圆胖的; 丰满的
13. neurotic [njʊəˈrɒtɪk] *adj.* unreasonably anxious or afraid, 神经质的, 神经病的
14. chortle [ˈtʃɔːt(ə)l] *vi.* to laugh, producing a sound that is halfway between a laugh and a snort, 咯咯地欢笑
15. wizened [ˈwɪz(ə)nd] *adj.* small and thin, with wrinkled skin, 干瘪的
16. shrivel [ˈʃrɪv(ə)l] *v.* to become shrunken or wrinkled, often by drying, (使)起皱纹, (使)枯萎
17. surly [ˈsɜːlɪ] *adj.* bad-tempered and unfriendly, 粗暴的, 乖戾的, 阴沉的, 无礼的, 板面孔的
18. fudge [fʌdʒ] *n.* a rich, soft candy made of sugar, milk, butter, and flavoring, 软糖: 一种柔软、甜腻的糖, 由糖、牛奶、奶油和香料制成
19. sundae [ˈsʌndeɪ; -dɪ] *n.* a dish of ice cream with a topping such as syrup, fruits, nuts, or whipped cream, 圣代冰淇淋
20. gooey [ˈguːɪ] *adj.* sticky and soft, 粘性的
21. crunchy [ˈkrʌntʃɪ] *adj.* crisp and and crackling when chewed, 发嘎吱嘎吱声的; 易碎的
22. blurry [ˈblɜːrɪ] *adj.* unclear in shape, 模糊的, 不清楚的
23. hazy [ˈheɪzɪ] *adj.* not clear or distinct in memory or in visual outline, 朦胧的, 烟雾弥漫的, 模糊的
24. blob [blɒb] *n.* a round mass of a liquid or sticky substance, 无一定形状(或难以名状)的一团东西
25. nebulous [ˈnebjʊləs] *adj.* unclear, without definite outline, 模糊不清的; 混乱的
26. tidbit [ˈtɪdbɪt] *n.* a small but interesting piece of information or news; small bit of food, 趣闻, 花絮; (美味食物的)一口

27. cholesterol [kəˈlestərɒl] *n.* a chemical substance found in blood, too much of which may cause heart disease, 胆固醇
28. clog [klɒg] *n.* an obstruction or hindrance, 阻碍, 障碍
29. fiddle [ˈfɪdl] *n.* violin, 小提琴
30. fiscal [ˈfɪsk(ə)l] *adj.* relating to money, taxes, debts, especially as administered by the government or other agency, 财政的
31. elusive [ɪˈl(j)uːsɪv] *adj.* difficult to describe or understand; avoiding capture, 难懂的, 难捉摸的
32. jigsaw [ˈdʒɪgsɔː] *n.* a picture cut into many interlocking pieces, 拼图玩具
33. mulch [mʌl(t)ʃ] *vt.* to put rotting leaves and twigs or manure around plants to protect and nourish them, 用覆盖物(或料)覆盖(地面、树木根部等)
34. boxwood [ˈbɒkswʊd] *n.* a kind of small evergreen tree with small shiny leaves, 黄杨树
35. brownie [ˈbraʊnɪ] *n.* a thick flat piece of dense chocolate cake, 核仁巧克力饼
36. torso [ˈtɔːsəʊ] *n.* human body, not including head, arms, or legs, (人体的)躯干
37. cerebral [ˈserɪbr(ə)l; səˈriːbr(ə)l] *adj.* intellectual and rational rather than emotional; of the brain, 聪明的; 用脑筋的
38. machination [ˈmækəˈneɪʃənz] *n.* secret, clever, and often unfair methods used to achieve an end, 阴谋诡计; 密谋
39. pat [pæt] *adj.* too quick, too simple, too easy, 非常恰当的; 预先准备好似的
40. loom [luːm] *v.* to appear as a large unclear shape, especially in a threatening way, 赫然耸现: 以放大的和有威胁性的形象出现在意识中
41. rutabaga [ˌruːtəˈbeɪgə] *n.* a long round yellow root vegetable, 芜菁甘蓝,〈美俚〉丑陋女人
42. downer [ˈdaʊnə] *n.* a depressing person or situation, 令人沮丧的人或境况
43. expound [ɪkˈspaʊnd; ek-] *vi.* to explain something in detail, 阐述, 说明
44. prognose [prɒgˈnəʊs, -ˈnəʊz] *v.* to predict the end result, 预测
45. probe [prəʊb] *v.* to ask questions, especially about personal matters; to poke around, 调查; 刺探
46. prick [prɪk] *v.* to make a small hole using something sharp, 刺, 戳
47. convivial [kənˈvɪvɪəl] *adj.* friendly and pleasantly cheerful, 好交际的; 快活的
48. acne [ˈæknɪ] *n.* an outbreak of pimples, usually on the face, 痤疮, 粉刺
49. gab [gæb] *vi.* to talk continuously, usually about something that is not important, 闲谈; 唠叨
50. giggle [ˈgɪg(ə)l] *v.* to laugh quickly, quietly, and in a high voice, often out of nervousness or embarrassment, 吃吃地笑, 以重复间歇的、短的声音笑
51. guffaw [gəˈfɔː] *vi.* to laugh loudly, 大笑
52. galumph [gəˈlʌmf] *vi.* to move in a noisy, heavy, and awkward way, 得意洋洋连跑带跳地行进; 脚步声嘈杂地行进; 笨拙地行进
53. gyrate [dʒaɪˈreɪt] *vi.* to whirl around in circles, 旋转
54. gluttonous [ˈglʌt(ə)nəs] *adj.* eating and drinking too much, 贪吃的
55. jiggly [ˈdʒɪglɪ] *adj.* moving in small rapid movements in any direction, 摇晃的; 不稳的

Unit Six

Useful Expressions

1. **goof off:** to waste time or avoid doing any work
   (1) My work duty is this afternoon, so I'm gonna goof off for a while.
   (2) They goofed off too much, and now they're not ready for the exam.

2. **clean up:** to make a place completely clean and tidy
   (1) We spent all Saturday morning cleaning up the mess from Saturday night.
   (2) There was mud all over the carpet, and it took me a long time to clean it up.

3. **spout off:** to talk a lot about something in a boring and annoying way
   (1) I really don't want to listen to Peter spouting off all afternoon.
   (2) All too often the old lady is spouting off about matters which should not concern her.

4. **hold up:** to raise, to keep raised
   (1) My husband has lost so much weight that he has to wear a belt to hold his trousers up.
   (2) You have held up your hand for some minutes. What do you want?

5. **reel off:** to recite a lot of information quickly and easily
   (1) Mary reeled off the titles of a dozen or so novels.
   (2) What is the point of teaching children to reel off the names of ancient kings if they know nothing of history?

6. **get a grip on oneself:** to act in a more sensible, calm, and controlled manner
   (1) Pull yourself together, my boy! You must get a firmer grip on yourself.
   (2) He has a good grip on himself and never gives way to anger.

7. **to be fit as a fiddle:** to be perfectly healthy
   (1) The man was almost ninety years old but fit as a fiddle.
   (2) Today she's as fit as a fiddle—thanks to research funded by efforts such as Beefy's.

8. **lead to:** to open the way for something to happen
   (1) A degree in English could lead to a career in journalism.
   (2) Disobeying the law could lead to trouble.

9. **off the mark / wide of the mark:** not correct, inaccurate
   (1) John didn't think the story was so far off the mark.
   (2) If that was meant to be an apology, your words were way off the mark.

10. **play it by ear:** to decide what to say or do in a situation on the spot rather than by following a plan
    (1) We'll see what the weather is like and play it by ear.
    (2) Devil Rays officials head to the winter meetings in Dallas this morning not sure exactly what they're looking for—they plan to play it by ear there.

11. **muddle through:** to reach an end point in an indirect and disorganized fashion
    (1) There were some difficulties, but I managed to muddle through.
    (2) I'm afraid I can't help you—you'll just have to muddle through on your own.

12. **have no use for:** to have no liking or respect for

    (1) I've no use for such old-fashioned methods. We must modernize at once.

    (2) The earnest young man had no use for jokes.

13. **whoop it up / whoop things up:** to enjoy oneself in a noisy and excited way

    (1) They whooped it up after winning the game.

    (2) Let's go to the party and whoop it up together!

14. **come up with:** to think of an idea or solution

    (1) Is that the best excuse you can come up with?

    (2) Thirty years ago, scientists came up with the theory that protons and neutrons are composed of three smaller particles.

15. **let somebody off the hook:** to allow or help somebody get out of a difficult situation

    (1) Robert has agreed to go to the party in my place so as to let me off the hook.

    (2) His opponents have no intention of letting him off the hook until he agrees to leave office immediately.

Understanding the Text

1. What does the title suggest about the thesis of the essay?
2. Is the author serious in speaking against thin people?
3. On the surface, the author is talking about the differences between thin people and fat people. But what is she really talking about?
4. In Paragraph 1, the author lists some characteristics of thin people and makes the comments that most of them are "menacing" and "All of them are dangerous." What image of thin people do you get from these? Why does the author say they are "menacing" and "dangerous"?
5. Describe the personalities of the "together" thin person and the "tsk-tsk" thin person.
6. What could be the "fat" sense of "goof off"?
7. What is the "way things actually are"? How do thin people and fat people "tackle" things differently?
8. What is the mystery of life? What could "the night" mean here?
9. In Paragraph 9, the thin person objects to the author's list. What is ironic about this objection?
10. What is the main problem with thin people? Why is it a problem?
11. In Paragraph 11, thin people's actions are described with several verbs all beginning with the letter "p" while in Paragraph 12, the author uses a series of words beginning with the letter "g" to describe fat people. What effects do these sounds achieve?
12. What is so attractive about the "fat" personality according to the last paragraph?

Unit Six

Exercises

A. Fill in the blanks with the appropriate words from the text.

1. Thin people have always got to be adoing. They should learn to _____. The author likes to surround herself with sluggish, inert, easygoing fat people, because thin people _____.

2. Thin people believe in logic. They stick to _____. They think their plans will _____ happiness. Fat people see all sides. The sides fat people see are _____ blobs, usually gray, always nebulous and truly not worth _____. Fat people realize that life is _____. They know happiness is _____ at best. They know all about the mystery of life. They are the ones acquainted with the night, with luck, with fate, with _____.

B. Choose from the words given below to complete the following sentences, changing the word form where necessary.

acquaint	come	eye	oppress	spring
arrange	ease	inert	quiver	tackle
bustle	elusive	loom	sluggish	vague

1. Some experts see this as a welcome opportunity to _____ the financial pressure.
2. The fear of a sudden attack _____ large in their minds.
3. He accused the cabinet of failing to _____ the severe economic and social problems in our country.
4. When she has a little spare time, she enjoys _____ her collected coins.
5. Success, however, remained _____ for him all his life.
6. Police said the thieves were obviously well _____ with the alarm system at the store.
7. The _____ shape of a figure loomed through the mist.
8. They no longer supply pretexts to _____, no reason for western governments to turn a blind eye.
9. A crowd of local children gathered around, _____ us in silence.
10. That famous Jamaican rum _____ in different colors, proofs, and ages.

C. Fill in the blanks with the phrases given below, changing the form where necessary.

clean up	hold up	reel off
come up with	lead to	spout off
goof off	muddle through	take in
stare at		

1. You'll never get your study done if you spend half your time _____.
2. Why doesn't somebody _____ places like this?
3. When the country boy visited the big city for the first time, all he could do was to _____ _____ the tall buildings in wonder.
4. He's not fit to be a chairman because he has a bad habit of _____ about things that concern him, without thinking of the results of what he says.

5. _____ your right hands and repeat these words after me.
6. It was a terrible mistake that could _____ disastrous consequences.
7. A methodical person is one who does things in a careful, orderly way; he doesn't _____ a job.
8. The teacher asked a difficult question, but finally Peter _____ a good answer.
9. He persuaded his grandparents to _____ him _____.
10. His wife _____ all his failings, whereas he was tongue-tied.

D. Fill in the blanks with the expressions given below, changing the form where necessary.

at least	lose track	get a grip on
off the mark	tight ships	the punch line
let sb. off the hook	have no use for	go straight to
fit as a fiddle	play it by ear	at best

1. This policy, they say, is _____ confused and at worst non-existent.
2. The manager _____ people who are always complaining.
3. If you can't come up with a plan, we'll have to _____.
4. _____ you can give him a call.
5. What you say is way _____.
6. His opponents have no intention of _____ until he agrees to leave office immediately.
7. Mary was so absorbed in reading that she _____ of time.
8. He told himself firmly to _____ himself.
9. As always, we _____ the experts for advice.
10. He didn't get _____ of the jokes.

E. Read the following text and choose the best word for each blank from the choices given.

The primary difference between men and women is that women can see extremely small quantities of dirt. Not when they're babies, of course. Babies of both sexes have a very (1) _____ awareness of dirt, other than to think it tastes better than food.

The opposite side of the dirt coin, of course, is sports. This is an area where men tend to feel very sensitive and women tend to be very (2) _____. I have written about this before and I always get (3) _____ letters from women who say they are the heavyweight racquetball (手球式墙球) champion of some place like Iowa and are sensitive to sports to the point where they could crush my skull like a ripe grape, but I feel these women are the (4) _____.

A more representative woman is my friend Maddy, who once invited some people, including my wife and me, (5) _____ to her house for an evening of stimulating conversation and cheerful companionship. (6) _____ sounds fine except that this particular evening occurred *during a World Series game*. If you can (7) _____ such a social mistake.

We sat around the living room and Maddy tried to stimulate a conversation, but we males could not (8) _____ our attention on the various suggested topics because we could actually feel the World Series television and radio broadcast rays zinging (发尖啸声) through the air, penetrating right into our bodies, causing our dental fillings to vibrate (振动), and all the while the women were (9) _____ *as though nothing were wrong*. It was exactly like that story by Edgar Allan Poe where the murderer can hear the victim's heart beating louder and louder, even though he (the murder victim) is dead, until finally he (the murderer) can't stand it anymore, and he just has to (10) _____ the World Series on television. That was how we felt.

1. A. high   B. good   C. poor   D. low
2. A. sensitive   B. casual   C. calloused   D. dull
3. A. appreciative   B. angry   C. thankful   D. sad
4. A. exception   B. example   C. occasion   D. case
5. A. into   B. at   C. over   D. in
6. A. That   B. It   C. What   D. Which
7. A. imagine   B. expect   C. suppose   D. think
8. A. attract   B. focus   C. distract   D. center
9. A. pretending   B. thinking   C. behaving   D. talking
10. A. see   B. view   C. look   D. watch

F. Translate the following sentences into English, using the phrases and expressions given in parentheses.

1. 国庆时,人们多爱去天安门广场欢呼庆祝。(whoop it up)
2. 他由于上班总是磨洋工而被开除了。(goof off)
3. 在我印象里,我妈妈总是不停地忙进忙出。(bustle)
4. 政府专门设立了一个特别工作组试图对付这个城市不断上升的犯罪率。(tackle)
5. 他经常滔滔不绝地说起他在部队时的有趣的事。(spout off)
6. 这个五岁小男孩能一口气说出一百来个国家的名称。(reel off)
7. 现在的问题是资金短缺,你所说的和这毫不相干。(off the mark)
8. 我们没法按计划进行,只能走一步看一步了。(play it by ear)
9. 我都不知道大学四年我是怎么稀里糊涂过来的。(muddle through)
10. 她说她受不了成天无所事事、到处闲逛的人。(have no use for)
11. 他总能找到迟到的借口。(come up with)
12. 我非常感激他帮我摆脱了困境。(let somebody off the hook)

Text B

Neat People vs. Sloppy People
Suzanne Britt

1. I've finally figured out the difference between neat people and sloppy people. The distinction is, as always, moral. Neat people are lazier and meaner than sloppy people.

2. Sloppy people, you see, are not really sloppy. Their sloppiness is merely the unfortunate consequence of their extreme moral rectitude. Sloppy people carry in their mind's eye a heavenly vision, a precise plan that is so stupendous, so perfect, it can't be achieved in this world or the next.

3. Sloppy people live in Never-Never Land. Someday is their metier. Someday they are planning to alphabetize all their books and set up home catalogs. Someday they will go through their wardrobes and mark certain items for tentative mending and certain items for passing on to relatives of similar shape and size. Someday sloppy people will make family scrapbooks into which they will put newspaper clippings, postcards, locks of hair, and the dried corsage from their senior prom. Someday they will file everything on the surface of their desks, including the cash receipts from coffee purchases at the snack shop. Someday they will sit down and read all the back issues of *The New Yorker*.

4. For all these noble reasons and more, sloppy people never get neat. They aim too high and wide. They save everything, planning someday to file, order, and straighten out the world. But while these ambitious plans take clearer and clearer shape in their heads, the books spill from the shelves onto the floor, the clothes pile up in the hamper and closet, the family mementos accumulate in every drawer, the surface of the desk is buried under mounds of paper, and the unread magazines threaten to reach the ceiling.

5. Sloppy people can't bear to part with anything. They give loving attention to every detail. When sloppy people say they're going to tackle the surface of a desk, they really mean it. Not a paper will go unturned; not a rubber band will go unboxed. Four hours or two weeks into the excavation, the desk looks exactly the same, primarily because the sloppy person is meticulously creating new piles of papers with new headings and scrupulously stopping to read all the old book catalogs before he throws them away. A neat person would just bulldoze the desk.

6. Neat people are bums and clods at heart. They have cavalier attitudes toward possessions, including family heirlooms. Everything is just another dust-catcher to them. If anything collects dust, it's got to go and that's that. Neat people will toy with the idea of throwing the children out of the house just to cut down on the clutter.

7. Neat people don't care about process. They like results. What they want to do is get the

Unit Six

whole thing over so they can sit down and watch the rasslin' on TV. Neat people operate on two unvarying principles: Never handle any item twice, and throw everything away.

8   The only thing messy in a neat person's house is the trash can. The minute something comes to a neat person's hand, he will look at it, try to decide if it has immediate use, and, finding none, throw it in the trash.

9   Neat people are especially vicious with mail. They never go through their mail unless they are standing directly over a trash can. If the trash can is beside the mailbox, even better. All ads, catalogs, pleas for charitable contributions, church bulletins, and money-saving coupons go straight into the trash can without being opened. All letters from home, postcards from Europe, bills, and paychecks are opened, immediately responded to, then dropped in the trash can. Neat people keep their receipts only for tax purposes. That's it. No sentimental salvaging of birthday cards or the last letter a dying relative ever wrote. Into the trash it goes.

10   Neat people place neatness above everything, even economics. They are incredibly wasteful. Neat people throw away several toys every time they walk through the den. I knew a neat person once who threw away a perfectly good dish drainer because it had mold on it. The drainer was too much trouble to wash. And neat people sell their furniture when they move. They will sell a La-Z-Boy recliner while you are reclining in it.

11   Neat people are no good to borrow from. Neat people buy everything in expensive little single portions. They get their flour and sugar in two-pound bags. They wouldn't consider clipping a coupon, saving a leftover, reusing plastic nondairy whipped cream containers, or rinsing off tin foil and draping it over the unmoldy dish drainer. You can never borrow a neat person's newspaper to see what's playing at the movies. Neat people have the paper all wadded up and in the trash by 7:05 a.m.

12   Neat people cut a clean swath through the organic as well as the inorganic world. People, animals, and things are all one to them. They are so insensitive. After they've finished with the pantry, the medicine cabinet, and the attic, they will throw out the red geranium (too many leaves), sell the dog (too many fleas), and send the children off to boarding school (too many scuff marks on the hardwood floors).

Exercises

Choose the correct answer to each of the following questions.

1. According to Britt, what is the major difference between neat people and sloppy people?
   A. Sloppy people are lazier than neat people.
   B. Neat people are meaner than sloppy people.
   C. Neat people are smarter than sloppy people.
   D. Sloppy people are more lovely than neat people.

2. Sloppy people are sloppy because _____.
   A. they have unachievable aims in this world

B. they are extremely morally correct

　　C. they always plan to do things someday

　　D. All of the above

3. How will sloppy people tackle the surface of a desk?

　　A. They will bulldoze the desk.

　　B. They will try to sort out everything on the desk.

　　C. They will leave it for some time later.

　　D. They will just do nothing about it.

4. Why are neat people very concerned about "results"?

　　A. They think results are more valuable than process.

　　B. Results mean more than process.

　　C. Results can show how neat they are.

　　D. They just want to get the whole thing over and sit down to watch TV.

5. How can people be neat?

　　A. Throw everything away.

　　B. Alphabetize all the books.

　　C. Clip all the coupons and save all the leftovers.

　　D. Treasure everything.

On-the-job Writing: Résumé

　　A résumé is a document that presents a brief summary of your educational background, work experience, professional skills, special qualifications, and honors; some résumés also contain a brief list of references. You may be asked to submit a résumé on a variety of occasions, most often to supplement your applications for jobs, interviews, promotions, scholarships, grants, fellowships, or other kinds of opportunities. Because prospective employers are the largest target audience for résumés, the following section offers advice to help job seekers design the most effective document possible.

　　Job seekers most frequently send their résumés with cover letters directed to particular employers. To prepare each cover letter, follow the basic steps for writing the traditional business letter. In the first paragraph, clearly tell your reader why you are writing: the specific job you are applying for and why. Devote one or more paragraphs in the "body" of your letter to noting your education or professional experience or both, explaining why you are a good match for the advertised position or how you might benefit the organization. Your concluding paragraph should express thanks for the employer's consideration and briefly reemphasize your interest in the job; in this paragraph you may also mention contact information or explain access to your credential file. In some situations, you may indicate your availability for an interview.

　　For the résumé, you might choose to adopt one of the two most popular styles:

- *Functional format:* This arrangement places the reader's focus more directly on the job seeker's education and skills than on limited work experience. It is better suited for job seekers who are new graduates or those just entering the work force. Most résumés of this type are one page.

- *Experiential format:* This style emphasizes professional experience by placing work history in the most prominent position, listing the current or most important employment first. This format might be best for nontraditional students whose work history precedes their education or for those students who have worked throughout their college careers. If the list of relevant professional experience is lengthy, this kind of résumé may extend to a second page when necessary.

Before you begin drafting your résumé, make a list of the information you want to include. Then think about the best ways to group your material, and select an appropriate title for each section. Some of the common content areas include the following:

1. **Heading.** Located at the top of your résumé, this section identifies you and presents your contact information: your full name, address, phone number, and e-mail address if you have one. You may wish to put your name in slightly bigger type or in bold letters.

2. **Employment objective.** Some job seekers choose to include a statement describing the kind of employment or specific position they are seeking. Others omit this section, making this information clear in their cover letter.

3. **Education.** It you have no relevant or recent work experience, this section might appear next on your résumé. Begin with the highest degree you have earned or are working on; if you are about to graduate, you may present the anticipated graduation date. Include the name of the school and its location and, if relevant, your major, minor, or special concentration. This section might also contain any professional certificates or licenses (teaching, real estate, counseling, etc.) you have earned or other educational information you deem relevant to a particular job search (internships, research projects, study-abroad programs, honors classes, or other special training).

4. **Professional experience.** If you wish to emphasize your work history, place this section after your heading or employment objective, rather than educational background. In this section, list the position title, name of employer, city and state, and employment dates, with the most current job or relevant work experience first. Some résumés include a brief statement describing the responsibilities or accomplishments of each position; you may list these statements (with "bullets," not numbers) or present brief paragraphs if space is an issue. If you include job descriptions, be specific (prepared monthly payroll for 35 employees) rather than general (performed important financial tasks monthly); use action verbs (supervised, developed, organized, trained, created, etc.) that present your efforts in a strong way. Use past tense verbs for work completed and present tense for current responsibilities.

Note that résumés traditionally do not use the word "I"; beginning brief descriptive phrases with a strong verb, rather than repeating "I had responsibility for...," saves precious space on a résumé.

5. **Skills.** Because you want to stress your value to a prospective employer, you may wish to note relevant professional skills or special abilities you have to offer. This section may be

especially important if you do not have a work history; many recent graduates place this section immediately following the education section to underscore the skills they could bring to the workplace. For example, you might list technical skills you possess or mention expertise in a foreign language, which might look useful to a company with overseas connections.

6. **Honors, awards, activities.** In this section, list those awards, scholarships, honors, and prizes that show others have selected you as an outstanding worker, student, writer, teacher, and so on. Here (or perhaps in a section for related skills or experiences) you might also add leadership roles in organizations, and even volunteer positions you have held, if mentioning these would further your case.

7. **References.** If references are requested with the initial application letter, the information may be listed at the end of the résumé or on an attached page. Reference information includes the person's full name and title or position, the name and address of the person's business or organization, telephone number, and e-mail address, if available. Do not list friends or neighbors as reference; résumé references should be academics or professionals who are familiar with your work.

Sample Résumé #1

Brent Monroe

417 Remington Street (970) 555-4567
Fort Collins, CO 80525 BCMonroe@aol.com

Education
B. S. in Business Administration, Colorado State University, May 2016. GPA 3.6
A. S. Font Range Community College, May 2014. GPA 3.9

Professional Skills
Accounting
    Spreadsheet programs
    Amortization schedules
    Payroll design and verification
    Contracts and invoices
Computer
    Word processing: Microsoft Word, WordPerfect
    Spreadsheets: Excel, Select
    Presentation: Powerpoint
    website design

Awards and Activities

Outstanding Student Achievement Award, College of Business, Colorado State University, 2016

President's Scholarship, Colorado State University, 2015 and 2016

Treasurer, Business Students Association, Colorado State University, 2016

Employment

Assistant Manager, Poppa's Pizza; Ault, Colorado, 06/2015—12/2016

References

Professor Gwen Lesser   Mr. Randy Attree

Department of Accounting   Manager, Poppa's Pizza

Colorado State University

Sample Résumé #2

ROSEMARY SILVA

3000 Colorado Avenue   (720) 555-6428

Boulder, Colorado 80303   Rosesilva@netscape.net

Objective

To secure a full-time position as an admissions counselor at a mental health or addiction recovery facility

Education

B. A. University of Colorado, Boulder, May 2016. Major: Psychology. Minor: Spanish. GPA: 3.5

Internship and Research Experience

Intern Detoxification Counselor, Twin Lakes Recovery Center, Boulder, Colorado; January—May 2016

Provided one- on- one counseling for in- patient residents; conducted admission interviews and prepared mental and physical evaluation reports; monitored physical vitals of patients; responded to crisis phone calls from out- patients; performed basic paramedical techniques; referred patients to other community agencies; supplied substance abuse information to patients and families.

Psychology Research Lab Assistant, University of Colorado at Boulder, under the direction of Professor Lois Diamond; September—December 2015

Helped conduct experiments on CU student-volunteers to measure the relationship of memory and academic success; explained experiment procedures, set up computers, recorded student information, validated research credit slips.

Employment

Night Security Dispatcher, University of Colorado, Boulder, Campus Police Department; May 2014—April 2016

Accurately received and responded to emergency and non-emergency calls and radio transmissions; communicated emergency information to appropriate agencies, such as Boulder Police and Rape Crisis Center; dispatched security units to handle crisis situations; wrote detailed records of incoming calls, security patrols, and responses.